悦读联播

Readaholic

英美文化读本

主　编　申立　　（英）詹姆斯·布兰沙德 等 　著
副主编　申蔷　　　　　　韩淑俊 等 　译

小学
第一册

中国盲文出版社

图书在版编目（CIP）数据

英美文化读本：大字版 . 小学 . 第一册：英汉对照 /（英）
詹姆斯·布兰沙德（James Blanshard）等著；韩淑俊等译 .
—北京：中国盲文出版社，2019.12
（悦读联播 / 申立主编）
ISBN 978-7-5002-9242-5

I.①英… II.①詹… ②韩… III.①英语—阅读教学—小
学—课外读物 IV.① G624.313

中国版本图书馆 CIP 数据核字（2019）第 239041 号

英美文化读本（小学第一册）

丛书策划：张世钦
责任编辑：张世钦　于　娟
责任校对：徐建春　顾　盛
出版发行：中国盲文出版社
社　　址：北京市西城区太平街甲 6 号
邮政编码：100050
印　　刷：东港股份有限公司
经　　销：新华书店
开　　本：787×1092　1/16
字　　数：130 千字
印　　张：14
版　　次：2019 年 12 月第 1 版　2019 年 12 月第 1 次印刷
书　　号：ISBN 978-7-5002-9242-5/G · 1086
定　　价：40.00 元
销售服务热线：（010）83190289　83190292　83190297

前言

　　学习英语必须了解英美文化，因为语言是文化的组成部分，是文化的载体，两者息息相关。大量事实表明，语言理解的障碍往往不在语言结构本身，而在相关文化知识的缺乏。何谓文化？从广义来说，文化是人类在社会和历史发展进程中创造的物质财富和精神财富的总和，包括文学、艺术、音乐、科学、技术、哲学、地理、建筑等。从狭义来说，文化是人们的生活方式、风俗习惯、行为准则等。所有这些，都需要用语言表达。英语有句名言：想要掌握两种语言，必须掌握两种文化。（To be bilingual, one must be bicultural.）英美文化对于广大的英语学习者的重要性可见一斑，而对于广大的一线英语教师来说，如果能够掌握广博的英美文化，不仅能够提升自己的文化素养，能够更加准确、传神地讲述教材，取得较好的教学效果，还能够进一步激发学生学习英语的兴趣和积极性，扩展他们的国际视野。

　　外研社基础教育出版分社经过长达四年的调查研究，广泛地听取了一线教师的意见，决定开发一套英美文化读本，以满足中小学英语教师的需求，并兼顾大专院校学生和一般读者的需求。为此，中方团队密切关注英美文化发展的最新态势，遵循国家《英语课程标准》的精神和中国学生学习英语的实际，提出选题方案，然后依据文章主题聘请各个领域的英美学者撰稿。在稿件完成后，中方专家又就内容和语言问题提出意见，请英美学者再进行修改和完善。

概括起来，这套读本具有以下特点：

一、内容充实，知识性和趣味性较强。这套读物涵盖了英美文化的诸多层面，从国情概况、国民性格、历史、地理、民族、建筑风格到民俗传统、文体生活、社会心态、旅游观光，向读者呈现出立体的、丰富多彩的英美社会风情。

二、材料新颖。这套读物对英美文化中出现的一些人和事作了介绍，譬如在谈及英国文化名人时，除了介绍影响力甚广的丘吉尔、达尔文、莎士比亚等历史人物，还介绍了人们非常熟知的英国球星贝克汉姆和流行歌手罗比·威廉姆斯等；又如小学读本 Clothing 一章，除了介绍服饰的历史发展和传统服装，还介绍了当代美国青少年中流行的着装风格等等。

三、语言规范。读者不仅可以多视角地熟悉英美文化，而且可以学到地道的英语。考虑到不同水平读者的需求，小学读本我们采取了中英对照的形式，以便读者准确理解文章的内涵。中学读本采取了注释的形式，对文中所涉及的具有特殊文化背景的内容加以解释，以便读者深入理解原文。

　　总之，我们相信，读者通过学习这套英美文化读本，将会提高跨文化交际的能力。书中疏漏之处，敬请读者不吝指教。

申　立

Preface

The world is getting smaller and smaller, but gaps between people have always existed and will continue to exist for the foreseeable future. Different sets of cultures, belief systems and values have shaped today's world. To avoid misunderstandings, we need to learn not only other languages, but the cultures behind the languages as well.

To understand English-speaking people, we first need to understand their culture and shared history and way of life. This series will give students a good general idea of life and culture in the United Kingdom and United States, helping them to fit in quickly if they visit. The articles in this series vividly depict the fabric of Western society from the perspectives of ordinary people—and their own experiences of life. As an American living in the United Kingdom, I am in a better position to know what's best about American culture through the eyes of my British friends, which I'm glad to share with you. Actually, all the articles in this series are written by native English speakers or authors who have lived in the West for a significant period. This ensures that the text presents an accurate picture of life in the English-speaking world.

As a children's publisher, I know that young students in particular need lively lessons that will engage their curiosity and desire to learn. Therefore, topics have been carefully chosen to include those of greatest relevance to children, including games, schools, clothes and festivals. The series also provides an interesting contrast of British and American culture, which gives you an insight into the differences between them and therefore enables you to better understand the two countries. Being aware that the teacher will pass on the information to students, the authors have made sure to present the text in a light-hearted and fun way, with interesting stories inserted where appropriate. This means that the series is a perfect fit for young Chinese students.

Mention should be made that the Chinese editors worked closely with the authors to make sure that the demands of the English curriculum were met. Where necessary, articles were carefully revised to meet the needs of the Chinese market.

British and American Culture Reader is not just another series, but a reflection of our society, a script being performed by the ordinary people in the two countries. Readers of this series will shake off some of the bad stereotypes that they hold about Westerners and may be surprised to find how similar Westerners' way of life is to their own in many ways. I hope you enjoy reading the articles as much as I have enjoyed writing them.

Nancy Dickmann

目录
Contents

1 **General introduction**
英美简介

2 **National leaders**
国家领导人

1 General introduction
英美简介

What is Great Britain?

James Blanshard

The United Kingdom of Great Britain and Northern Ireland, to call it by its full name, is a nation in Western Europe. We call it the UK for short. The people that live in England, Scotland, Wales and Northern Ireland are called 'British' and the language spoken by people in Britain is English. In Wales, some people speak the Welsh language, and you can see road signs in Welsh and English if you go there.

People visit the UK from all over the world. There are some important towns and cities there, and also lots of farmland. The land is good for raising sheep and cows, as well as for growing vegetables and crops, like potatoes and wheat. Some parts of the UK are mountainous. The highest mountain in the UK is called Ben Nevis, which is in Scotland. There are some nice sandy beaches, forests and marshland too.

In the past, all sorts of people lived in the UK. The Romans invaded 2000 years ago and lived there for about 400 years. The Romans called the nation Britannia, after a goddess that was worshipped there. The name 'Great Britain' comes from that Roman name. They built many of the cities in England that are still there today, and you can find Roman remains in many places in the UK. Some of the best remains are the Roman baths in the city of Bath, and parts of Hadrian's Wall, which separated the Roman lands from Scotland.

In 410 AD, the Romans left the country, and there came a time people call the 'Dark Ages'. Many tribes from neighbouring countries wanted to live in Britannia and so there were lots of invasions and battles. The Dark Ages lasted around 600 years. Invading tribes of Angles, Saxons, and the fearsome Vikings all conquered parts of the country in the Dark Ages. It was around this time that the name England first came to be used. It means 'Land of the Angles'. Also in those days, the first kings of England ruled. You can read about some of those kings in later chapters of this book.

The last people to conquer England were the Normans

(from France) in 1066, after they won the famous battle of Hastings. The wonderful Bayeux tapestry, which is kept in France, shows the history of that famous battle. The history of the British Parliament dates back to Norman England too. Parliament is a group of elected and chosen people that make the nation's laws. Today, they meet in the Houses of Parliament in London, and at other places in Scotland and Wales.

The different people that have ruled Britain have all brought their own languages and ways of life. This is one of the reasons why the English language has some unusual words and customs! Some common words have lots of different meanings. Did you know that the *Oxford English Dictionary* has over 40 definitions for the words 'round' and 'light' and over 70 for the word 'run'? This can make learning English a tricky task!

Today, around 67 million people live in the UK, and most of the people live in England. The UK's biggest cities are in England, but there are important cities in Scotland, Wales and Northern Ireland too. Some British cities, like London, Edinburgh, Manchester, Oxford and Nottingham are famous around the world for many different reasons. Some are well known for their sports team (like Manchester United football club), their university (like Oxford), their arts and music festival (like Edinburgh), or famous people that lived there in the past (like Robin Hood in Nottingham).

Look out for these groups, people and places as you read through this book!

英国简介

韩淑俊 译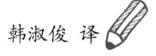

　　大不列颠及北爱尔兰联合王国是一个西欧国家的全称，我们将其简称为英国。住在英格兰、苏格兰、威尔士和北爱尔兰的人通称"英国人"，他们所使用的语言是英语。在威尔士，有些人讲威尔士语。要是你去那儿的话，你会看到那儿的路标是用威尔士语和英语两种语言标注的。

　　世界各地的人到英国参观访问。英国有一些重要的城镇，还有大量的农田。那里的土地适宜养殖牛羊、种植蔬菜以及土豆和小麦之类的农作物。英国有些地方是山区，最高的山峰是本尼维斯山，位于苏格兰。此外，英国还拥有美丽的沙滩、森林和沼泽地。

　　历史上形形色色的人都在这片土地上居住过。两千年前罗马人入侵英国，并在英国生活了约 400 年。古罗马人称这个民族为"不列颠（Britannia）"——当地人所供奉的一个女神的名字。"大不列颠（Great Britain）"就是由此演变而来的。罗马人在英格兰建造了许多城镇，这些古老的城镇留存至今。如今你在英国的很多地方都能找到古罗马遗迹。保存最好的遗迹包括巴斯市的罗马浴池和横亘于古罗马帝国领土和苏格兰之间的哈德良长城的残余部分。

公元 410 年，罗马人离开英国，"黑暗时代"开始了。邻国许多部落都想到不列颠居住，由此引发大量入侵活动和战争。"黑暗时代"持续了约 600 年。在此期间入侵的部落包括盎格鲁人、撒克逊人，还有可怕的维京人，他们先后征服了这个国家的部分领土。正是在这个时期，"英格兰 (England)"这个名字首次得到使用。它的意思是"盎格鲁人的土地"。也正是在这个时期，英格兰最早一批国王开始统治这片土地。本书后面的章节会向读者介绍他们当中的几位。

1066 年，来自法国的诺曼人在著名的黑斯廷斯战役中取得了胜利，成为最后一批征服英格兰的入侵者。保存在法国的、精美的贝叶挂毯就展现了这一著名的战役。英国议会的历史也可以追溯到诺曼人统治时代。议会由一群被选举和挑选出的代表组成，他们负责制定国家法律。如今，议会在伦敦的议会大厦以及苏格兰和威尔士的其他一些地方举行会议。

历史上曾经统治不列颠的民族带来了自己的语言和生活方式。这正是英语中存在着一些特殊词汇和惯用法的原因之一！有些常用词有很多不同的含义。你是否知道《牛津英语词典》中对"round"和"light"的释义有40多个，而"run"的释义有70多个？这无疑使英语学习成为了一项棘手的任务！

　　现今，约有6700万人住在英国。英国最大的城市和主要的人口都分布在英格兰，但是苏格兰、威尔士和北爱尔兰也有一些重要的城市。英国的一些城市，如伦敦、爱丁堡、曼彻斯特、牛津和诺丁汉，基于不同的原因闻名于世：或是因为它们的体育团队（如曼彻斯特联队足球俱乐部）、大学（如牛津大学）、艺术和音乐节（如爱丁堡），或是因为曾在那里生活的名人（如诺丁汉的罗宾汉）。

　　读者在阅读本书的时候，不妨留意一下这些团队、人名和地名！

The land of Scotland

Kenneth and Joan Cameron

Scotland, known in the past as Alba and Caledonia, is a small country. It is only 78,772 square kilometres in area and has a population of around 5.4 million. However, Scottish people can be found in almost every part of the world and many of them have made a significant contribution to the good of the countries that they have moved to. Scotland has been described in boxing talk as 'punching above its weight'. This means that it has made a big impact on the world relative to its small size.

Scotland is one of the four entities that make up the United Kingdom of Great Britain and Northern Ireland. The others are England, Wales and, of course, Northern Ireland. Although for centuries Scotland shared a queen and government with the rest of the United Kingdom, the Scottish people have always felt that they are a separate nation from England. Scotland's own kings ruled until the year 1603 when a Scottish king was made the English king (James I).

From that time there was only one king, who ruled from England, over both countries. In 1707 the Scottish and English parliaments became one. But even in these circumstances, Scottish affairs were dealt with by a separate department until almost 300 years later when, in 1998, Scotland was granted a parliament of its own again to deal with its internal affairs. This Scottish parliament still answers to the UK parliament as it cannot collect its own taxes, but there are many Scottish people who want to change that and who want Scotland to become an independent country once more.

The Scottish landscape is mainly one of mountains and moorland and open wetlands, inland lochs (the Scottish word for 'lakes') and beautiful rivers. On the western side, the mountains sweep down fairly close to the shore and the shoreline is indented by many inlets and arms of the sea (these are known as sea lochs or sea lakes). The eastern seaboard is less mountainous. Most of the fertile, arable land of the country is to be found there and in the Central Lowlands, which is a broad stretch of lower land across what might be regarded as the waistline of the country. Most of the Scottish population and four of the country's six cities are situated in these Central Lowlands where much of Scotland's economic wealth is generated and along the more level eastern countryside. There is a much sparser population in the Highlands, especially around the western shoreline and in the island groups of the west and north.

Between the Central Lowlands and the boundary with England is a large area known as the Scottish Borders. Here, smooth rounded hills, less rugged than the northern mountains, present a gentle landscape that is the setting for a number of towns in attractive river valleys.

The border with England is a very significant line. Today there are no border posts and passage from one side to the other is free, but it was not always so. When the mighty Roman army swept across Europe and invaded Britain, they managed to occupy England and Wales but not Scotland. After 80 AD the Romans tried to cross the Scottish border many times but were fought off by the local people and turned back. So the Romans built a wall from east to west across the north of England to keep the wild Scots out. Thus the northern limit of the Roman Empire was in the north of present-day England.

But who were these warring tribes who were able to keep the powerful Romans out of their territory? The Romans named the main group who confronted them Picts, meaning painted people. This was on account of the purple war paint they wore in battle. However, the origins of the present population of Scotland (with the exception of more recent immigrants) is a mix of different groups known as Picts, Gaels, Brythons, Angles, Norsemen and Celtic peoples who eventually, through the passage of time, collectively became known as Scots. The name Scot seems to come from a Gaelic (Celtic) tribe from Ireland who originally settled in Scotland's southwest in around 450 AD. Today the term Scot is used to describe all Scottish people.

Historians travelling through Scotland can trace evidence of early races and their different cultures. Stone circles, burial mounds and ancient carved stones tell of different tribal religions, cultures and customs. Another example is the many place names in the north and northern islands, such as Laxdale, Lerwick and Seaforth that reveal colonisation by Norsemen or Vikings from Scandinavia. In the Western Isles and parts of the mainland, the Gaelic language is still used and is a living link with the great Celtic 'empire' that existed in this area.

This multi-ethnic mix of peoples bonded together as a single nation—the Scots—with the reputation of being an industrious, enterprising, enquiring and inventive people. They are known worldwide because they can be found in almost every country, usually reminding others of their presence by Scottish celebrations of different kinds.

Many Scots had a hand in the birth of modern nations, for example, Canada and the USA. Also, by discovery and invention, the Scots contributed much to the development of life as we know it today. No one will research the origins of television, pneumatic tyres, the bicycle, the telephone, the hydrofoil, gas lighting, kerosene (paraffin), the steam engine and waterproof fabric without finding the hand of Scotsmen therein. The Scottish also contributed to endeavours such as the development of radar and the cloning of sheep and in the medical field, to the discoveries of penicillin, cures for various tropical diseases, chloroform's anaesthetic qualities and beta blockers. In the field of economics, Adam Smith of Kirkcaldy was the first real international political economist who wrote *The Wealth of Nations* and has had a profound influence on economic thinking.

With Scotsmen being the inventors, discoverers, founders and chief developers of so much that shapes our lives for the better today, the statement that Scotland 'punches above its weight' is definitely true.

苏格兰概况

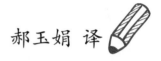

郝玉娟 译

　　苏格兰在历史上曾被称作阿尔巴和喀里多尼亚，是一个面积仅有 78,772 平方公里、人口约 540 万的小国。但是苏格兰人却遍布世界几乎各个角落，且其中不少人为他们所在的国家作出了卓越的贡献。借用拳击术语来说，苏格兰是一个"出拳能量超出身体重量"的国家，这里暗喻苏格兰虽然国家不大，但对世界的影响却巨大。

　　苏格兰是组成大不列颠及北爱尔兰联合王国的四个实体之一，其他实体包括英格兰、威尔士，当然，还有北爱尔兰。尽管几百年来，苏格兰和英国其他三个实体一样服从英国女王和英国政府的管辖，但是苏格兰人一直觉得他们与英格兰是两个不同的国家。1603年，苏格兰国王继位成为英格兰国王，即詹姆士一世；而在那之前，苏格兰一直由自己的国王统治。自那以后，由住在英格兰的一个国王统治两个国家。1707年，苏格兰与英格兰议会合二为一。但即使在这样的情况下，苏格兰的事务也一直由一个单独的部门处理。直到近 300 年后的 1998 年，苏格兰再次获准成立了自己的地方议会来处理其内部事务。苏格兰议会仍然向联合王国议会负责，因为它无权收税，但是许多苏格兰人想改变这种情况，谋求苏格兰的再次独立。

苏格兰的自然景观以山地、高原沼地、开放的湿地、内陆湖泊和美丽的河流为主。在苏格兰的西部地区，山峦绵延至海岸，那里的很多入海口与狭长水湾（被称为海湖）使海岸线呈犬牙交错之势。比较之下，东部沿海地区地势则较为平缓，苏格兰的大部分富饶的耕地就位于这里以及被称作中央低地的一片横跨苏格兰腹地的开阔低地。苏格兰的大部分人口和苏格兰六个城市中的四个都分布于这片经济发达的中央低地和地势较为平坦的东部乡村，而苏格兰高地的人口则稀少得多，特别是西部海岸线一带及西部和北部的群岛。

在中央低地与苏格兰和英格兰边境的中间是一大片被称为苏格兰边境的地区。这里平滑浑圆的山丘不像北部高地那样突兀。在这片较为平缓的地区，一些小镇散落在美丽的河谷中。

苏格兰与英格兰的边界线极为重要。今天，那里没有边境检查站，双方的来往通行也不受限制，但过去可并非如此。强大的罗马军团横扫欧洲并入侵英国时，罗马人成功占领了英格兰和威尔士，但对苏格兰却束手无策。在公元 80 年后，罗马军团曾数次试图跨过苏格兰边境，却遭到了当地人的顽强抵抗，最后无功而返。为了避免强悍的苏格兰人来找麻烦，罗马人在英格兰北部建造了一道横贯东西的城墙。因此，罗马帝国的北部边界位于今日英格兰的北部。

但是，究竟是哪些能征善战的部族把强大的罗马人拒之境外？罗马人把与其正面交锋的主要族群称作皮克特人，即涂了颜色的人。这源于该族群在交战时脸上涂的紫色颜料。然而，除新移民外，目前的苏格兰人是由皮克特人、盖尔人、布立吞人、盎格鲁人、古斯堪的纳维亚人和凯尔特人等不同族群随着时间的推移逐渐融合而成的。"Scot（苏格兰人）"这个名字似乎源于一个盖尔（凯尔特）部落的名字，这个来自爱尔兰的部族最初于公元 450 年前后住在苏格兰西南地区。今天，"Scot"被用来称呼所有的苏格兰人。

游览苏格兰的历史学家可以发现这些早期族群以及他们不同的文化所留下的痕迹。石圈、墓冢以及古代石刻都记述了不同部落的宗教、文化及风俗习惯。北部地区和北部岛屿的许多地名如拉克斯戴尔、勒威克和锡福斯，表明它们曾是古斯堪的纳维亚人或维京人的殖民地。而在苏格兰西部诸岛和部分大陆地区，盖尔语仍在使用，它像一条纽带，联系着这里曾经存在过的、伟大的凯尔特"帝国"。

这是一个由多民族融合在一起组成的单一民族——苏格兰。苏格兰人遍布全球，以勤劳、进取、善于探究和创新闻名于世。他们通常用各种各样的具有苏格兰特色的庆祝活动来提醒世人他们的存在。

许多苏格兰人参与缔造了一些现代国家，如加拿大和美国。另外，他们的发现和发明对我们现今拥有的生活贡献巨大。任何人在调查电视、充气轮胎、自行车、电话、水翼艇、煤气照明、煤油、蒸汽发动机和防水面料的起源时，都会发现其中有苏格兰人的参与。在雷达的研发、绵羊克隆以及在医学领域内青霉素、各种热带疾病的治疗方法、氯仿的麻醉质量、β-受体阻滞药的发现方面，苏格兰人也功不可没。在经济学领域，《国富论》的作者（苏格兰）柯卡尔迪人亚当·斯密是第一位真正的国际政治经济学家，对于经济思维有着深远的影响。

如此多的发明和发现极大地改善了我们今天的生活，而苏格兰人作为发明者、发现者、创建者和主要研发人员，印证了小小的苏格兰"出拳能量超出身体重量"绝非浪得虚名。

America

Nancy Dickmann

The United States of America is a large country in North America. Many people call it the US, USA, or just 'America'. It is made up of 50 separate states that each have their own government, capital and laws. However, the national government, based in Washington, D.C., oversees many aspects of daily life. The main language in the USA is English, although many other languages are spoken. Over 40 million people speak Spanish, which is the second most popular language.

Geography

The USA is the fourth largest country in the world, and it stretches about 3000 miles from east to west. Two main mountain ranges run north to south through the country: the Rocky Mountains in the west, and the Appalachian Mountains in the east. Between them, great rolling prairies stretch for hundreds of miles. Here, farms grow huge crops of wheat and corn. The area is nicknamed 'America's

Breadbasket'. In the southwest corner of the country, the land is more like a desert, with many weird and wonderful rock formations such as the Grand Canyon. The United States also includes Hawaii, a group of islands in the Pacific Ocean, and Alaska, a huge wilderness that extends into the Arctic Circle.

History

The first people to live in the United States were the Native Americans, sometimes called 'Indians'. These people lived in many tribes scattered across the land. The first European settlers arrived in the 16th century. By 1775, the British controlled a string of colonies along the east coast. The colonists began to get angry with the British taxes, and they started a war of rebellion. They won the war, and in 1783 they became an independent country.

After independence, the country grew quickly, and its borders soon extended all the way to the west coast. There were only 13 states at the beginning. Over the years, more and more were added as the country grew. Millions of immigrants came to the United States from other countries. They hoped to have a better life than they had had in their own country. America was called the 'land of opportunity', and although life was hard for the immigrants, many of them did succeed in their goal. Even today, American culture, language and food show the influence of these immigrants. The country is often called a 'melting pot' because different cultures have mixed together, like the ingredients in a stew or soup!

One of the symbols of America is 'Uncle Sam'. This character is an old man with a white beard, who wears clothes that look like the American flag. He is based on a real person who supplied food to the army in the 1800s.

America today

More than 300 million people now call the United States home. Many of them live in cities or suburbs, but there is also a sizeable rural population. The country is made up of regions that often have their own accent, food and culture. The northeast part of the country is called 'New England'. It has some of the oldest settlements and a large Irish-American population. The southeast is often called just 'the South'. This area has a large African-American population. Many of these people are descended from the African slaves who once worked the farms. Louisiana is home to a group called 'Cajuns'. The area was originally settled by French-speaking people from Canada, and touches of French language and culture still remain.

The Midwest is an area known for its large farms. The West is where the legend of the cowboy started, and there are still many ranches and rodeos. Some people wear cowboy hats! California is famous for Hollywood and for its beautiful scenery and coastline.

Although the people in different regions of the United States may speak and act differently, they all share a sense of the nation's history and values. Americans are all proud to be American!

美　国

张艳波 译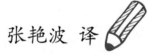

　　美利坚合众国是北美洲的一个大国，许多人简称其为美国。美国由 50 个州组成，各州均有自己的政府、首府和法律，而位于华盛顿特区的联邦政府负责监管国家日常生活的众多方面。美国人使用多种语言，但主要语言还是英语。西班牙语是第二大语言，讲西班牙语的人数超过 4000 万。

地理

美国是世界第四大国，东西绵延约 3000 英里（4800 多千米），两条主要山脉贯穿南北：落基山脉位于西部，东部的是阿巴拉契亚山脉。两大山脉之间是绵延起伏数百英里的大草原，这里的农场盛产小麦和玉米，号称"美国粮仓"。美国西南隅地形接近沙漠，有许多奇异的岩石结构，如大峡谷。美国领土还包括太平洋上的夏威夷群岛以及延伸至北极圈的阿拉斯加荒原。

历史

美国原住民即土著美国人，有时被称为"印第安人"。他们分成很多部落，散居在美国各地。第一批欧洲殖民者于 16 世纪到达美国。截至 1775 年，英国已经在美国东海岸拥有一系列殖民地。殖民者开始对英国的税收感到愤怒，进而发起反抗战争。最后他们取得胜利，并于 1783 年成为了一个独立的国家——美国。

独立之后，美国迅速扩张，它的领土边界一直延伸到了西海岸。最初，美国只有 13 个州，但是随着国家的发展壮大，州的数量越来越多。数百万移民从其他国家来到美国，希望在这里生活得更好。美国号称"机会之地"，虽然移民在这里生活很艰辛，但许多人的确都成功实现了自己的目标。即使现在，美国文化、语言和食物依然显示着这些移民的影响。美国常被称为"大熔炉"，因为它融合了世界各地不同的文化，就像炖菜或汤里包含了各种原料一样。

"山姆大叔"是美国的象征之一，此人的形象是一位长着白胡子、身着类似美国国旗图案衣服的老人。这个人物的原型是19世纪美国军队的一个食品供应商。

今日美国

现在，美国人口超过三亿，多数人居住在城市或郊区，但住在乡村的人也相当多。美国分为不同区域，每个地区都有自己的口音、食物和文化。东北部称为"新英格兰"，那里有最古老的定居点，居住着大量爱尔兰裔美国人。东南部通常简称"南部"，那里生活着很多非洲裔美国人，他们中许多人是从事农场劳动的非洲奴隶的后代。路易斯安那州是卡金人的居住地，这里原本住的是讲法语的加拿大人，直到现在，法语及法国文化对这里的影响依然存在。

中西部以大农场著称。西部是牛仔传奇的发源地，现在那里仍然有许多大牧场和牛仔竞技表演，有些人依然戴着牛仔帽！加利福尼亚因好莱坞和美丽的风景及海岸线而著名。

尽管美国不同地区的人们言行举止可能不尽相同，但他们拥有同样的国家历史感和价值观，并且都以自己是美国人而感到自豪！

British and American influence

Nancy Dickmann

America is often called 'the world's only remaining superpower', so it is no surprise that its influence is felt around the world. But Britain, although it is a much smaller country, also has significant influence. Both countries have made their mark in the world through diplomacy, but also through culture.

America and Britain were both founding members of the United Nations, and they are permanent members of the Security Council. This means that both countries wield great power in international affairs. Although other countries may not always agree with their ideas or actions, they are taken seriously around the world.

Britain's history helps to explain why such a small country can have such a wide influence. For hundreds of years, it ruled an empire that stretched around the world. Although nearly all of its former colonies are now independent countries, many of them still have links to Britain. The Commonwealth of Nations is an organisation made up of more than 50 of these countries. They have joined together to promote common interests such as world peace, equal rights, and democracy.

In the modern world, news and information are now available worldwide, and much of this information comes from either Britain or America. This helps spread British and American ideas and opinions too.

However, one of the most noticeable types of influence is cultural influence. British and American culture has spread around the world through film and television. The latest Hollywood blockbusters can be seen in all corners of the globe, either in cinemas or on DVDs or videos. Famous film characters such as Indiana Jones or James Bond are known around the world. Television programmes also travel widely. Some, such as *Baywatch*, are shown in their original form. Others are adapted to individual markets. A good example of this is the quiz programme 'Who Wants to Be a Millionaire?' This was originally a British programme, but there are now over 70 international versions of the show, each one slightly different.

Sports stars such as David Beckham and teams such as Manchester United have fans from many different areas. Their matches can be seen on satellite television almost everywhere you go.

Popular music from the English-speaking world travels to every corner of the globe, especially with the Internet and downloadable music. Literature from authors such as Shakespeare and even J. K. Rowling is translated into many languages. And art by British and American artists can be found in galleries around the world.

American food and fashion have travelled the world. Products such as Coca-Cola, Starbucks' coffee and McDonald's hamburgers can be found almost everywhere you go. Economists have even invented something called the 'Big Mac Index'! This calculation compares the purchasing power of different countries by looking at the price of a Big Mac in each market. Western influence can also be felt in large-scale changes. For example, many people in China now drink more milk, at least partly because this type of Western diet is seen as desirable.

American fashion such as blue jeans has been popular at least since World War II. During the Cold War, when anything American was seen as suspicious in the Soviet Union, young people would smuggle in blue jeans and sell them on the black market. Now blue jeans are widely available, and for many people they are still the height of cool. But they have become so popular around the world that many people no longer see them as American!

英美的影响力

张艳波 译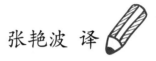

　　美国经常被称为"世界现存的唯一超级大国"，因此，全世界都受其影响就不足为奇了。然而，英国虽然比美国小得多，却也有着举足轻重的影响力。英美两国通过外交和文化使世界感受到它们的影响。

　　英美两国都是联合国的创始会员国，也是安全理事会常任理事国，这就意味着两国在国际事务中有很大的影响力。尽管其他国家未必总是赞同英美的意见或行动，但它们会得到慎重对待。

　　英国的历史有助于说明为何这么小的国家能有如此广泛的影响。几百年来，大英帝国在全球范围内扩张。尽管几乎所有的英国前殖民地目前都已独立，但是它们中的许多依然和英国保持着联系。英联邦就是由 50 多个这样的国家组成的组织，它们联合起来促进共同利益，如世界和平、平等权利和民主。

　　当今世界，新闻和资讯在全球范围内传播，而许多信息都来自英国或美国，这也有助于英美思想观念的传播。

然而，文化的影响是最显著的影响之一。英美文化通过电影、电视传播到全球。世界各地的人们都可以通过电影院、DVD 和录像看到最新的好莱坞大片。著名的电影角色如印第安纳·琼斯和詹姆斯·邦德闻名全球。电视节目也得到广泛传播，以《海岸救生队》为代表的节目原版播出。其他节目则稍作改动，以适应各地市场的个性化需求，智力竞赛节目《谁想成为百万富翁？》就是一个很好的例子。起初这是一档英国节目，但现在全球已有 70 多个版本，每个版本都略有不同。

　　体育明星如大卫·贝克汉姆和运动队如曼联在许多不同的地区都有球迷，无论你在哪里，都能通过卫星电视观看到他们的比赛。

　　英语国家的流行音乐能够传播到世界每个角落，特别是借助于互联网和音乐下载的力量。英语文学作品，如莎士比亚以及 J.K. 罗琳的作品被译成多种语言。英美艺术家的作品在世界各地的美术馆都能看到。

　　美国食品和时尚传遍了全球。无论在哪里，你几乎都能看到美国食品，如可口可乐、星巴克咖啡和麦当劳汉堡包。经济学家甚至发明了"巨无霸指数"！这种计算方法通过"巨无霸"在各地的价格差别来比较不同国家的购买力。我们还可以在大规模的变化中感受到西方的影响，譬如现在中国许多人喝牛奶比以往多，至少部分原因在于这种西方饮食方式看起来更可取。

以牛仔裤为代表的美国时尚至少从二战时就已经很流行。冷战期间，苏联对美国的任何东西都持怀疑态度，年轻人则把美国的牛仔裤偷偷运进国，并在黑市上出售。现在，牛仔裤已经风靡全球，对很多人而言，它依然是最酷的。但是，因为牛仔裤在全球如此风行，许多人不再认为它是美国的时尚。

2 National leaders
国家领导人

Famous kings and queens

James and Kate Blanshard

There have been many kings and queens of England and later of Britain, but before the year 927 there was no single ruler of England. Ever since then, Britain has had a royal family, and all sorts of brave, and sometimes scary, kings and queens!

England has been invaded many times. Perhaps the most famous invader came from northern France. In the year 1066, hundreds of boats filled with soldiers and horses led by William of Normandy made their way from France across the sea to England. In the famous battle of Hastings, William's army fought against the English soldiers and eventually beat them! William became King William I of England. He is better known as 'William the Conqueror'.

Richard I was King of England from 1189 to 1199. He is known as 'Richard the Lionheart' because he was a brave leader, and commanded his own army at the age of just 16! Although he is famous as an English hero, Richard did not actually spend much time in England because he was abroad fighting most of the time.

There have been some cruel kings in England's history. When King Edward IV died in 1483, his son Edward, who was 12 years old, was next in line to be king. However, young Edward and his nine-year-old brother were taken to the Tower of London by their uncle Richard. Their uncle declared that the boys' parents had not been properly married, and that he was therefore the new king of England, King Richard III! The princes were never seen alive again. What exactly happened to them is a mystery, but most people think that Richard III had them killed to make sure that they did not threaten his position as King.

In 1491, one of England's most famous kings came to the throne. Henry VIII was a large man who enjoyed hunting and music. He had six wives, although not all at the same time! Henry was desperate to have a son who could take over as king when he died. For this and other reasons, he got rid of several of his wives so that he could marry again and again, either by divorcing them or by ordering them to be executed!

Henry did have a son, Edward, but he was very ill and did not live long after Henry's death. However, Henry's daughter became Queen Elizabeth I, and she ruled for 44 years. Elizabeth never married, and is well-known as having bright orange hair and very pale white skin. She was queen at the time William Shakespeare first staged his plays in London.

Later, in 1649, one of the most famous events in British history took place. After many years of war within England, Parliament signed the death warrant of King Charles I. They ordered the execution of the king! King Charles I was beheaded and his family fled to France. England was run by Parliament under the leadership of Oliver Cromwell. Oliver Cromwell was very strict. He banned colourful clothes, closed down the theatres, and even stopped people celebrating Christmas! In 1660, England had had enough, and they decided to call back Charles's son, who was also called Charles, to be King Charles II.

As we come into the 1700s and more modern times, we reach King George III. Although George III is probably best known for losing America and for his struggle with mental illness, he was a popular king and a loyal family man. George III's marriage to Sophia Charlotte of Mecklenburg-Strelitz was arranged, and the couple only met on their wedding day! However, George was devoted to his wife, and they had 15 children. George encouraged learning and the arts. He built a collection of about 65,000 books, which were later given to the British nation, and founded the Royal Academy of Arts. George III is also thought to have donated more than half of his personal income to charity.

Then we meet Queen Victoria, who was famous as one of the longest reigning female monarchs. She ruled Britain for 63 years, from 1837 to 1901! She was devoted to her husband, Prince Albert, and they had nine children. When Albert died in 1861, she spent many years mourning him. For the rest of her life she wore only black clothes as a sign of how much she missed him. Queen Victoria's reign brought in lots of British traditions, such as white wedding dresses and Christmas trees.

There are a lot more interesting stories about British kings and queens than we have space for here! Do you know who the current British monarch is?

著名的国王和女王

黄菲飞 译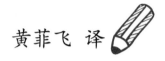

早期的英格兰到后来的英国（即大不列颠及北爱尔兰联合王国）有很多国王和女王。然而在公元 927 年之前，英格兰并没有一个统一的统治者。从那以后，英国拥有了一个王室，并出现了许多或勇敢、或残暴的国王和女王。

英格兰曾多次遭到外来入侵，其中最著名的入侵者来自法国北部。1066 年，诺曼底公爵威廉率领着满载战士和战马的船队从法国渡海登陆英格兰。在著名的黑斯廷斯战役中，威廉率领的诺曼底军队最终击败了英格兰军队，威廉成为英格兰历史上著名的国王威廉一世，他更为人们所熟知的称谓是"征服者威廉"。

理查一世在 1189 年到 1199 年间是英格兰国王，因其骁勇善战而被称为"狮心王理查"，他年仅 16 岁时就已经开始统帅自己的军队。虽然理查一世是一位著名的英国英雄，但他在英格兰所呆的时间却少之又少，因为他绝大部分时间都是带着军队在国外征战。

在英格兰历史上也有一些残暴的国王。1483 年，国王爱德华四世去世后，理应由其年仅 12 岁的儿子爱德华继承王位。然而，年幼的爱德华和他年仅 9 岁的弟弟却被他们的叔叔理查关进了伦敦塔。理查宣称这两个孩子的父母的婚姻不合法，因此将由他自己继承王位并成为理查三世。人们从此之后再也没有见到过两位小王子的身影，其间到底发生了什么也成了一个谜，但大多数人认为理查三世为了确保自己的王位不受威胁而杀死了两位小王子。

1491 年，英格兰历史上最著名的国王之一 —— 亨利八世即位。亨利八世块头很大，喜欢狩猎和音乐。因为十分渴望能有一个儿子在自己死后继承王位，亨利八世先后娶了 6 位妻子。由于子嗣的问题和其他原因，亨利八世通过离婚或处死的方法先后摆脱自己的几位妻子，从而能够一而再再而三地娶妻。

亨利八世后来确实有了一个叫爱德华的儿子，然而爱德华体弱多病，在亨利八世去世后不久也一命呜呼了。随后，亨利八世的女儿即位成为女王，即伊丽莎白一世，她统治英国长达 44 年。伊丽莎白一世终身未婚，她因为一头鲜亮的橙色秀发和异常苍白的肤色而为世人所知。她在位期间，威廉·莎士比亚的戏剧首次在伦敦上演。

随后，在 1649 年，一件英国历史上最著名的事件发生了：在英格兰多年内战后，英国议会签署了死刑执行令，下令处死国王查理一世！查理一世被斩首后，他的家人流亡到法国。奥利弗·克伦威尔成为英格兰护国公，通过议会管理英格兰。奥利弗·克伦威尔十分古板严厉，他不许人们穿颜色艳丽的服装，关闭了所有的剧院，他甚至禁止人们庆祝圣诞节。到1660年时，英格兰人民再也无法忍受奥利弗·克伦威尔的统治，他们决定召回名字也叫查理的查理一世的儿子，加冕他为国王查理二世。

当我们走进18世纪和更现代的英国时，就不得不提到国王乔治三世。虽然人们最熟知的或许是乔治三世在施政期间失去了美洲殖民地和其饱受精神错乱的折磨，但乔治三世是一位深受民众爱戴的国王，也是一位忠于家庭的男人。乔治三世和来自梅克伦堡－施特雷利茨的索菲娅·夏洛特的婚姻是包办婚姻，夫妇两人在婚礼上才平生第一次见面，但乔治三世对自己的妻子十分忠诚，他们共同抚育了15个孩子。乔治三世还鼓励学习和发展艺术，他收藏了6.5万册图书（后将这些书赠予国家），并创建了英国皇家艺术学院。据传乔治三世还将自己一半以上的个人收入捐给了慈善机构。

接下来我们要谈一谈英国在位时间最长的君主之一，并因此闻名于世的维多利亚女王，她从1837年到1901年共统治英国长达63年之久。她和丈夫阿尔伯特亲王感情甚笃，共抚育了9个孩子。1861年阿尔伯特亲王辞世后，维多利亚女王长年郁郁寡欢，哀悼丈夫的辞世。在之后的岁月里，女王终其一生都身着黑色服饰，以表达对丈夫的无限哀思。维多利亚女王的统治给英国带来了许多新的传统，比如白色的婚纱和圣诞树的出现。

关于英国国王和女王的有趣故事还有许多，我们这里篇幅有限，就不一一累述了。你知道现在的英国君主是谁吗？

Royal traditions

James and Kate Blanshard

Britain's monarchs lead busy lives! Let's follow a monarch, Queen Elizabeth II, through a typical year to see what royal traditions she follows.

At the start of each year, and again in June, the monarch issues an honours list. This is a list of people who will receive a special award to recognise their services to the country. This could be because they have been very good at sport, or because they are great actors or politicians. When you have been honoured, you are given a new title. A woman can be made a 'Dame' and men may be knighted. When a man is given a knighthood, he can put 'Sir' before his name. When the Queen gives a knighthood, the man being knighted kneels in front of her and she uses a sword to touch his shoulders.

The months have passed and it is Easter time. The Thursday before Easter Day is called Maundy Thursday. Each year on Maundy Thursday the Queen visits a different cathedral to go to the Maundy

Thursday service. At the service, she gives out special coins, called 'Maundy money' to elderly people chosen from around the area. This tradition is over 1000 years old!

Imagine how amazing it would be to have two birthdays every year. In 2006, Queen Elizabeth II celebrated her 80th birthday on April 21 and again on June 17! She was actually born on April 21, 1926, but since the reign of King Edward VII in the early 1900s the public celebration has been in June. This tradition began so there was a chance the weather would be better!

On the birthday in June there is a special military parade of royal guards, who march past and salute the monarch. This is called the 'Trooping of the Colour'. It dates back a long time to when flags, also known as colours, were marched in front of the soldiers so that they learnt what their flags looked like and could recognise them in battle.

The Queen also sends letters to some people on their birthday. However, you have to wait until you reach 100 years old to get one!

In late October or early November each year, the monarch is involved in opening parliament. The Queen wears a crown and special robes. She travels down the road from Buckingham Palace to the Houses of Parliament in a golden carriage. When the carriage arrives, the Union Jack flag is taken down in the Houses of Parliament and the monarch's flag, called the royal standard, is put up in its place.

The Houses of Parliament are made up of the House of Commons and the House of Lords. In 1642, King Charles I marched into the House of Commons with his guards to arrest five members of parliament. Since then, no monarch has been allowed to enter the House of Commons. So, the Queen goes to the House of Lords and sends a messenger, called 'Black Rod', to the House of Commons. Black Rod has to knock three times before the House of Commons let him in. The Queen sits on a throne and reads her speech, which today is usually written by the government.

December 25 is Christmas Day! Every year on Christmas Day the Queen gives her Christmas speech to the nation. She talks about what has happened during the year, giving a message to her people. Lots of supporters all around the country watch her on the television. It has been another busy year for the Queen and it is all about to start again!

英国王室传统

黄菲飞 译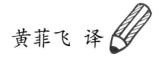

英国君主们的日子过得可真是忙碌！下面就让我们跟随女王伊丽莎白二世一起去看看，一年之中她都遵循了哪些王室传统。

在每年的年初和 6 月份，英国君主会颁布一份嘉奖名单，名单上列出的人士都会因其对国家作出的突出贡献而获得特殊嘉奖。这些获奖人士有的可能在体育界成绩斐然，有的在演艺界声名显赫，也有的在政界政绩突出。被嘉奖的人将获得一个新的头衔，一般女士受封为"女爵士"，男士受封为"爵士"。男士被册封为爵士后，他可以在名字前冠以 Sir（爵士）的头衔。当女王册封爵士时，受封者跪在女王面前，女王会用一把剑去触碰受封者的双肩。

每年的前几个月一过，就到复活节了。复活节之前的那个星期四被称为"濯足节"。每年的濯足节，女王都要去一个不同的大教堂参加"濯足节"礼拜。在礼拜活动中，女王会把一种叫做"濯足节币"的特殊银币赠予那些从当地挑选出来的长者，这一传统已经延续了 1000 多年。

　　想象一下：要是一年能过两次生日该多好！ 2006 年，女王伊丽莎白二世就分别在 4 月 21 日和 6 月 17 日庆祝了两次自己的八十大寿。她实际上是在 1926 年 4 月 21 日出生的，但自从 20 世纪初国王爱德华七世开始，王室官方的生日庆典都定在 6 月举行，这一传统的形成是因为在 6 月份，庆典活动可能会赶上个比较好的天气。

　　在 6 月份的生日庆典上会举行一场特殊的皇家卫队游行活动，皇家卫队的士兵们步履整齐地从女王面前走过并向女王行军礼，这一活动也被称为"军旗敬礼分列式"。"军旗敬礼分列式"起源于很久以前的战争时期，当时军旗（flags，也称为 colours）被举在行军队伍前方，这样士兵们得以牢记旗帜的样子，从而在战斗中通过辨识军旗认清自己的队伍。

　　女王也会给一些过生日的人寄去贺信，但你如果想得到一封这样的信，就必须得等到一百岁的时候。

　　每年的 10 月末或者 11 月初，君主都要参加议会开幕典礼。女王带上王冠，并穿上特制的礼服，乘坐一辆金色的马车从白金汉宫抵达议会大厦。当女王的马车抵达时，议会大厦的英国国旗降下，女王使用的皇家旗徐徐升起。

　　英国议会由下议院和上议院组成。1642 年，国王查理一世带着他的皇家卫队闯进下议院并逮捕了五名议员，自此以后，英国议会禁止君主进入下议院。因此，女王直接到达上议院，并派出一位被称为"黑杖侍卫"的信使前往下议院，而这位黑杖侍卫必须用黑杖在下议院门前敲三下才会被允许进入下议院。女王坐在王位上宣读她的文告，而这些文告现在通常都是由英国政府起草的。

12月25日就是圣诞节了。每年的圣诞节，女王都会向全国民众发表圣诞讲话。在讲话中，女王会谈及过去的一年中发生的事情，并向国民奉上贺词。英国许多的女王支持者都会在电视前关注女王的讲话。对女王而言，可真是又忙碌了一年啊，而新的一年又将开始啦！

The royal family

James and Kate Blanshard

The British royal family is the close family of the British monarch. People usually become King or Queen because they were born into the royal family and were the next in line after the previous King or Queen. The next in line is called the 'heir to the throne'. The crown usually passes to the eldest son. If the King or Queen has a daughter she will only be the heir to the throne if she does not have any brothers. If she has brothers, even if they are younger than her, the oldest brother will be the heir. King George VI had two daughters and no sons. When he died, his eldest daughter became Queen Elizabeth II. Queen Elizabeth II's first child was a son, Charles, so he became heir to her throne.

The monarch is called His or Her Majesty. Close members of the monarch's family are called His or Her Royal Highness, or 'HRH'. Some members of the monarch's family have special titles. The monarch's eldest son is given the title 'Prince of Wales'. This dates back to 1301, when King Edward I conquered

Wales and gave this title to his heir, Prince Edward. Since the 1400s the second son of the monarch has usually been given the title 'Duke of York'. If the Duke marries, his wife is called the 'Duchess of York'. Younger sons of the monarch are usually made a Duke when they get married. A monarch's eldest daughter is often given the title 'Princess Royal'.

Until modern times, the King or Queen of Britain had a family name instead of a surname. This referred to the 'house' or family that their father was from. Queen Victoria married Albert, who was from the German House of Saxe-Coburg-Gotha. So, their children and grandchildren belonged to that house too. Victoria's grandson, King George V, was king when the First World War started in 1914. Britain fought against Germany, so British people did not like German names and words. In 1917, George V decided to stop using the German titles that he and his family had. He decided his family should have a surname instead and picked the name Windsor, after Windsor Castle. However, even today, the monarch and their close family do not need to use their surname. When they put their signature on something they only sign their first name.

The royal family has an important role to play in helping the monarch with their national duties. They often attend events or travel to meet people around the world, when the monarch is not able to. The monarch welcomes guests from Britain and abroad to their British homes. For example, every year there are at least three Royal Garden Parties at Buckingham Palace with about 8000 guests at each party. In total, the monarch welcomes about 70,000 people each year at dinners, lunches, and garden parties! The royal family help the monarch by attending and hosting these events. The royal family also receive and answer about 100,000 letters every year.

Members of the royal family have their own role to play that is separate to the monarch. Several members of the royal family have served in the Royal Navy, Air Force or Army. The royal family organise and take part in local events around Britain, such as opening new buildings or attending celebrations. The royal family also do charity work. About 3000 charities list a member of the royal family as their supporter. Sometimes members of the royal family set up their own charities. For example, Queen Elizabeth II's son, The Prince of Wales, set up a charity called The Prince's Trust which helps young people from difficult backgrounds.

The royal family is very popular all around the world, and wherever they visit there is always a crowd of people to greet them!

英国王室

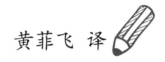

黄菲飞 译

　　英国王室指的是英国君主的直系亲属。国王或女王的继承人通常出生于王室，并且是王位的第一顺位继承人。这位第一顺位继承人被称为"王储"。英国的王位通常会传给长子，只有当国王或女王没有儿子的时候，才会把王位传给他们的女儿。如果公主有兄弟的话，就算兄弟比她小，王位依然会传给长子。比如说：国王乔治六世只有两个女儿而没有儿子，所以当他去世之后，他的长女就继承王位，成为了女王伊丽莎白二世。女王伊丽莎白二世的第一个孩子是个儿子，即查尔斯王子，在这种情况下，查尔斯王子就成了英国王储。

　　君主被尊称为"国王陛下"或"女王陛下"，君主的直系亲属被尊称为"殿下"，有些王室成员还拥有特殊的头衔，比如君主的长子都被赐予"威尔士亲王"的头衔。这一头衔的来历可以追溯到 1301 年，那一年英国国王爱德华一世征服了威尔士，并把"威尔士亲王"这一头衔赐予其王位继承人爱德华王子。自 15 世纪以来，君主的次子通常都被赐予"约克公爵"的头衔。如果约克公爵结婚了，那么他的妻子就被称为"约克公爵夫人"。君主其他年龄较小的孩子一般在他们结婚后会被赐予"公爵"的头衔，而君主的长女通常被授予"长公主"的头衔。

近代以前，英国的国王或女王使用王朝姓氏，而不使用私人姓氏。王朝姓氏能够表明家族里的父辈们所属的王朝或皇族。维多利亚女王与来自德国萨克森—科堡—哥达王朝的阿尔伯特结婚后，他们的子孙们都沿用这一王朝姓氏。1914年第一次世界大战爆发时，维多利亚女王的孙子——乔治五世是当时的英国国王。因为英国当时与德国交战，所以英国人不喜欢德国的姓名或词语。1917年，国王乔治五世决定停止使用他及家族成员所拥有的德国王朝头衔，并决定从此以后其王室开始使用私人姓氏，他选用了温莎城堡名字中的"温莎"。然而，时至今日，英国君主和王室成员并不需要使用他们的私人姓氏，他们签字时只需要签上自己的名字就可以了。

王室成员在辅佐君主完成公务方面发挥了十分重要的作用。当君主无暇参加一些活动或去世界各地访问时，王室成员常常代替君主履行这些职责。英国君主在王宫中招待来自英国本土和世界各地的宾客，例如：王室每年都在白金汉宫举行至少三场皇家花园游园会，每次前来参加的宾客都有8000人左右。如此算来，英国君主每年在各种晚宴、午宴和游园会上总共要招待的宾客大约有 70,000 人之多！王室成员们通过参加或举办这些活动的方式来协助君主。他们每年收到并回复的信件总数也达到十万封之多。

　　除了王室公务，王室成员还有各自重要的事务要处理。有些王室成员服役于皇家海军、空军或陆军。王室成员还会组织和参加英国各地的地方性活动，比如出席一些建筑物的落成典礼或各地的庆祝活动。王室成员还致力于慈善工作，约有 3000 个慈善组织将王室中的某一成员列为他们的支持者。有些王室成员还建立了自己的慈善组织，比如女王伊丽莎白二世的儿子威尔士亲王就建立了一个叫做"王子信托基金会"的慈善组织，旨在帮助那些来自困难家庭的年轻人。

　　王室成员在全世界都极受关注和欢迎，无论走到哪里，都会获得成群结队的人们的问候。

US presidents

Nancy Dickmann

The United States has never had a king or a queen. Instead, every four years the people elect a president to lead the country. The president is the head of state, which means that he represents his country to other leaders around the world. But the president is also the leader of the country's government, as well as being commander-in-chief of the armed forces. It is a very busy job!

Presidential elections

Anyone can run for president, as long as they are at least 35 years old and were born in the United States. They must also have lived in the US for at least 14 years. But once you've met these requirements, there is still a long way to go! Elections are held every four years. Each political party can nominate one candidate for president, and the two biggest parties are the Democrats and the Republicans. Over the course of several months they will whittle down the list of hopefuls until they choose the person who will be their candidate.

The presidential election is held on the first Tuesday of November, every four years. Most US citizens who are at least 18 years old can vote. They go to a polling place in their local area and cast their ballot. However, it is a group of only 538 people who actually elect the president! They are called the Electoral College. Each state is assigned a certain number of electors, based on the population. When a person votes for the president, they are actually voting for an elector who has promised to vote for that candidate.

Once the votes are counted and the winner is declared, everyone prepares for the inauguration. This ceremony is held on 20 January of the following year. The new president and vice-president take an oath to uphold the Constitution and carry out their jobs properly. After that, it's time for a party! There are dozens of Inauguration Balls held in Washington, D.C., and the new president and his wife make an appearance at half a dozen or so.

Presidential traditions

The president and his family live in the White House, a large mansion in Washington, D.C. This building also has offices for the president and his staff. A specially modified airplane called Air Force One carries the president to meetings and appearances all over the world. The president also has his own helicopter, called Marine One. He even has his own song! At many public appearances, a march called 'Hail to the Chief' is played when he enters.

Aside from government work, the president has many public duties. At Easter, he and his wife host an Easter egg roll on the White House lawn for local children. Traditionally, the president throws out the first pitch at the start of the baseball season each year. At Thanksgiving, a holiday that is celebrated with a turkey dinner, he delivers an official pardon to one turkey. And in December each year, he switches on the lights on the National Christmas Tree.

Famous presidents

The United States has had over 40 presidents, but some have a special place in history. George Washington was elected as the nation's first president in 1789. He is often called the 'Father of His Country' and is remembered especially for having false teeth! Thomas Jefferson was the third president, and although he was a great president, he was also interested in many other things. He was a gardener, an architect, a scientist, an inventor, and a writer. He also founded the University of Virginia. Abraham Lincoln was president during the American Civil War, when the country almost split in two. He kept the nation together and also passed a law to free the slaves. In 2009, Barack Obama made history by becoming the first black president.

美国总统

黄菲飞 译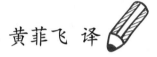

美国的历史上从来没有过国王或者女王，但是美国民众每四年会选举出一位总统来领导国家。美国总统是国家元首，在世界其他领导人面前代表着美国，他同时也是美国政府首脑和三军统帅 —— 总统的工作可真是够忙的！

总统选举

任何一位出生在美国、年满 35 周岁、并已在美国居住 14 年以上的美国公民都可以参加总统竞选。不过，仅满足上述这几个条件还是远远不够的。选举每四年举行一次，每个政党可以提名一位本党总统候选人。美国最大的两个政党为民主党和共和党。各政党需要用几个月的时间逐渐淘汰有希望成为总统候选人的人选，并最终选定一位代表本党的总统候选人。

每四年举行一次的总统大选在 11 月的第一个星期二举行，绝大多数年满 18 周岁的美国公民都可以参加投票。他们会到当地的投票站投下自己的选票。实际上，真正投票选出总统的是被称为"总统选举团"的 538 名选举人。美国各州都按照其人口数量而分配到相应的选举人名额，当一位美国公民投票选举总统时，他实际上是把票投给了该州的一位选举人，而该选举人承诺把选票投给选民支持的那位总统候选人。

一旦统计完选票数量并宣布了获胜者，人们就开始为总统就职典礼做准备。总统就职典礼于下一年的 1 月 20 日举行，新当选的总统和副总统宣誓将捍卫美国宪法并忠实履行各自的职责。就职典礼结束后将举行庆祝宴会。在华盛顿特区会有数十场庆祝总统就职的舞会，新任总统和他的夫人将会出席其中的大约六场。

与总统相关的传统

总统及其家人住在白宫。白宫坐落在华盛顿特区，是一座宏伟的官邸，其中有总统及其工作人员的办公室。总统会乘坐一架经过特别改装的"空军一号"专机去世界各地参加各种会议和露面。他拥有自己专属的直升机"海军一号"，他甚至还有自己专属的歌曲！在很多公众场合，只要总统一露面，"向统帅致敬"的进行曲就会响起。

除了处理政府事务外，总统还要参与很多公众活动。在复活节的时候，总统偕夫人在白宫草坪为当地的孩子举办滚彩蛋的活动；每年的职业棒球赛季开始时，总统都要按照传统为比赛开球；每逢感恩节人们都要吃火鸡大餐时，总统则要颁布特赦令特赦一只火鸡；每年 12 月份的时候，总统还要开启国家圣诞树上的彩灯。

几位著名的总统

迄今为止，美国一共有过 40 多位总统，其中的一些在历史上占有特殊地位。1789 年，乔治·华盛顿当选为第一任美国总统，人们经常把他称为"国父"，他还因为戴假牙而让人们印象深刻。托马斯·杰弗逊是美国历史上的第三任总统。他是一位杰出的总统，同时具有广泛的兴趣，是一位园艺家、建筑师、科学家、发明家和作家，还创建了弗吉尼亚大学。亚伯拉罕·林肯是美国内战时期的总统，当时美国面临一分为二的危机，他捍卫了国家的统一，并颁布法律解放了奴隶。2009 年，贝拉克·奥巴马创造历史，成为美国历史上的第一位黑人总统。

Family
家庭

A British wedding day

James Blanshard

A traditional Christian wedding service in the UK might be a bit like this...

It's a sunny summer Saturday afternoon. The church is full of ladies in their finest dresses and hats. The men are wearing their smartest suits and the children are on their best behaviour. The guests are chattering quietly—a little nervously—in the church pews. It's almost time for the service to begin!

At the front of the church is the most nervous man of all. His knees are weak and his throat is dry, but his family and friends are around him to wish him well. He's the Groom, and today is his wedding day!

Suddenly, a hush falls on the church. Near the doors, the guests whisper excitedly to one another: "She's here! She's here!" They crane their necks to get their first glimpse of the Bride.

The music starts and all eyes turn to the doors. Walking down the aisle of the church, arms linked with her proud father, is the Bride in a beautiful white dress. She walks slowly and carefully, hoping she can say the right words and stay calm. Behind the Bride follow her Bridesmaids, also wearing beautiful matching dresses.

The wedding ceremony has begun. The Bride and Groom make promises to love and care for each other. They exchange wedding rings. Hymns are sung and prayers are offered, and then comes the moment they have been waiting for... the minister declares them husband and wife!

After the service, everybody is happy and smiling, and the church bells ring in celebration! A crowd gathers outside the church as the Bride and Groom leave, and the guests throw a shower of confetti into the air over them. The 'happy couple' are so relieved that they're finally married, and now everyone wants to wish them well and take photographs.

There's now a time for formal photographs and

the two families pose for pictures. The Bride's grandmother reminds her of the old poem 'Something old, something new, something borrowed, something blue!' Tradition says that if the Bride wears all of these things today her marriage will be lucky. And of course, the Groom made sure he never saw his Bride's wedding dress before they met in the church.

Now, a special car drives up and the Bride and Groom wave goodbye to the crowd. Soon, they are guests at their wedding reception—a special party held in their honour.

There, the Best Man, who is a dear friend of the Groom, gives a cheeky speech and everybody laughs. The Bride's father and the Groom give speeches too, thanking everyone for their friendship and kind gifts.

Then, a tasty meal is served and the Bride and Groom cut their wedding cake—there's a slice for everyone. Finally, to start the evening dancing, the couple have their 'first dance' as husband and wife. It's a nervous moment, but soon everybody joins them on the dance floor.

The bride now turns her back and an excitable crowd gathers behind her. Her friends jostle for position, but why? Suddenly, she throws her bouquet of flowers over her head into the crowd! Hands reach up and one lucky girl catches the flowers—tradition says she'll be the next girl to get married...

It's been a very emotional day! There've been lots of tears of joy and happiness. Now, finally, when it's getting late, the wedding car arrives again to whisk the Bride and Groom away on their honeymoon holiday. There are some tearful goodbyes to the happy couple, and the party is over. The day is finished, but it won't be forgotten.

Not all weddings in the UK are like this. Many people from other countries with different customs live in the UK too, so as well as Christian weddings like this one, there are Jewish, Islamic, Hindu and Buddhist weddings, and weddings that have no religious vows. These are all quite different, but they are all usually wonderful celebrations!

英国婚礼一日记

韩淑俊 译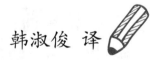

　　传统的英国基督教婚礼仪式可能会是这样一幅情景……

一个夏日周六的午后，阳光灿烂。教堂里挤满了穿着最漂亮的衣服和戴着精美礼帽的女士们。男士们则穿着最帅气的西装；孩子们表现得也十分乖巧。客人们坐在教堂的长椅上窃窃私语，略显紧张。婚礼马上就要开始了！

　　在教堂里，站在前面的那个男子是最紧张的。他的腿发软，喉咙发干，而他的家人和朋友们围在他的身边祝福他。他就是新郎，今天是他举行婚礼的大喜日子！

　　突然，教堂里安静了下来，靠近门口的宾客兴奋地互相低语："她来了！她来了！"他们都伸长脖子，想要一睹新娘的容貌。

　　音乐响了起来，所有人的目光都投向了门口。新娘身着美丽的白色礼服，手挽着为她深感自豪的父亲，沿着教堂中间的过道走了过来。她的步伐缓慢而谨慎，希望自己能够言语得体，保持冷静。紧随其后的是伴娘，她们漂亮的礼服与新娘的礼服相得益彰。

　　婚礼开始了。新娘和新郎承诺要给予彼此真爱与关怀，然后他们交换结婚戒指。接着，大家一起吟唱赞美诗和吟诵祈祷词。之后，新人一直等待的时刻终于到来了——牧师宣布他们结为夫妻。

　　婚礼仪式结束了，每个人都很高兴，脸上洋溢着微笑，教堂响起庆祝的钟声！当新娘和新郎离开的时候，人们聚集在教堂外面，向新婚夫妇头顶抛洒五彩的纸屑。这"幸福的一对"总算松了口气，他们终于结婚了。此刻，人们都期望为他们送上祝福，并与他们一起拍照。

这时到了正式拍照的时间，两家人都摆好拍照的姿势。新娘的祖母提醒她要记得那首古老的诗歌"有旧、有新、有借、有蓝"。依照传统，如果新娘今天的穿戴里包括所有这些东西，她的婚姻将会很幸福。当然，还有在教堂相见之前，新郎必须保证不能看到新娘的礼服。

此时，一辆专用婚车开了过来，新娘和新郎与众人挥手告别。而不久之后，这些宾客会出席他们的婚宴，即他们为答谢来宾而举办的宴会。

在宴会上，伴郎，也就是新郎最好的朋友，发表了一通"放肆"的讲话，每个人都笑了起来。新娘的父亲和新郎也分别讲话，以感谢朋友们的情意和友好的礼物。

然后，美味的饭菜上桌了，由新娘和新郎一起切结婚蛋糕，并分给来宾们每人一块。最后，宴会跳舞时间到了，先由这对新人跳他们成为夫妻后的第一支舞。这是一个紧张的时刻，但是很快大家也都来到舞池中与他们共舞。

新娘这时候转过身，一群兴奋的人聚集在她身后。她的朋友们争相找好位置，这是为什么呢？突然，新娘将一束花抛过头顶，扔向人群中！大家都伸手去接，一个幸运的女孩接住了这束花。按照传统说法，她将会是下一个结婚的女孩……

这是激动人心的一天！有很多喜悦和幸福的泪水。这时天色已晚，婚车再次驶来，载着新娘新郎开始蜜月之旅。人们向这对甜蜜的新人含泪告别，同时宴会就此结束。这一天过去了，却令人难以忘怀。

在英国，并非所有的婚礼都是这样。有许多其他国家的人也住在英国，他们有不同的结婚风俗，所以既有像这样的基督教婚礼，也有犹太教、伊斯兰教、印度教和佛教婚礼，另外也有一些没有宗教誓言的婚礼。这些婚礼虽然大不相同，但同样都是精彩的庆祝活动！

Family life in the UK

James Blanshard

Family life in the UK can be very varied. People from lots of different cultures live in the UK, so families can be big and small. They can live in big houses with large gardens or in very small apartments with no gardens at all.

A typical British boy or girl in the UK lives in a house in a town with their mum and dad, and one or two brothers or sisters. Pets are very popular in the UK so many homes will also have a cat or dog, which is treated like part of the family.

Grandparents sometimes live with their families, or will often live close by. This means that the family can meet up easily to have meals together or visit one another when they need help. Many grandparents look after their grandchildren and help with childcare while parents go to work.

Let's imagine a typical day in the life of a British schoolboy. His name is Jack and he lives with his mum, dad and younger sister, Emma. Jack is 9 years old and Emma is 7. They have a pet dog called Max.

It's Thursday morning—a school day. At about 7:30 a.m., Jack and Emma's mum puts her head around the bedroom door and tells them it's time to wake up and get ready for school. If Mum and Dad are lucky, Jack and Emma will jump out of bed straight away. If not, they will let Max into the room to lick their faces to wake them up. Max is always pleased to see them!

After they have been to the toilet and had a wash, Jack and Emma head downstairs for breakfast. They have toast and breakfast cereal. Dad is already dressed for work. He works in an office as a town planner. Mum is dressed for work too. She works in a school.

After breakfast, Mum and Dad help the children get dressed. The children take a packed lunch to school, which Mum and Dad make for them before they leave for work. They are also given some pocket money to buy some sweets as a treat at lunchtime.

Dad leaves for work because he has to catch a train to get to his office. Jack and Emma give him a hug before he leaves. Mum drives the children to school and drops them off in a street nearby so they can walk the rest of the way—it gets very crowded at the school gates in the morning!

Jack and Emma enjoy school because they can play with their friends, and they like learning. Jack especially enjoys playing football at lunchtime, and Emma likes painting pictures.

After school, the children are met by their grandmother at the school gates. Jack and Emma call her 'Nana' for short. They walk back to Nana's house and have some tea before Mum drives round to collect them. At Nana's house, they watch television for a little while or maybe for a treat they can play games.

When they get home the family eats an evening meal. The children then finish any homework they have, and if the weather is good they join Dad as he takes Max for a walk.

Finally, if they've been well behaved and all the homework is finished, they may be allowed to play some video games before bedtime.

By 9 o'clock, Jack and Emma are in their pyjamas and tucked up in bed. Mum and Dad are reading them bedtime stories. Jack and Emma like magical adventure stories, so there are lots of good ones to choose from.

Tomorrow is Friday, and they can start to look forward to the weekend! Mum and Dad will take them to the swimming baths on Saturday morning, and they will have lots of time to do fun things they enjoy, like playing football in the garden with Max!

英国家庭生活

张艳波 译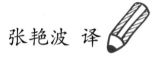

英国人的家庭生活多种多样。居住在英国的人来自不同的文化背景，所以他们家庭的规模大小不一。他们既可能生活在有大花园的豪宅里，也可能住在没有花园的小公寓里。

英国孩子通常和他们的父母以及一两个兄弟姐妹一起住在城镇的房子里。英国人很喜欢养宠物，所以许多家庭还会养一只宠物猫或狗，人们对待宠物就像对待家人一样。

祖父母有时会与子孙同住，或者住得离他们很近。这样便于家庭聚餐或在需要帮助的时候彼此照应。通常祖父母会在子女上班时帮忙照看孙子孙女。

让我们想象一个英国学生日常生活中的一天吧。他叫杰克，与父母和妹妹艾玛同住。杰克今年9岁、艾玛7岁。他们有条宠物狗，名叫马克斯。

这是周四早上——这天是上学的日子。早上七点半，杰克和艾玛的妈妈把头探到卧室门口，叫他们起床准备上学。如果运气好的话，杰克和艾玛会马上从床上跳下来。但如果他们不起床的话，父母就会让马克斯跑过去舔他们的脸，把他们叫醒。马克斯总是很高兴见到他们！

在卫生间洗漱完毕之后，杰克和艾玛就会下楼去吃早餐。他们早餐吃烤面包片和早餐麦片。这时，爸爸已经穿好衣服准备去上班了，他在办公室任职，是一位城镇规划员。妈妈也已经穿好衣服准备上班，她在学校工作。

孩子们吃过早饭后，爸爸妈妈帮他们穿好衣服。爸爸妈妈在上班之前还为孩子们准备好了午餐便当，让他们带上，并且会给他们一些零用钱，以便他们在午餐时间可以买些糖果来款待自己。

爸爸出门了，他要赶火车去上班。杰克和艾玛在爸爸离开之前拥抱了他。而妈妈则开车送他们去学校，她在学校附近的一条街道把他们放下，让他们自己走过去——因为早上校门口的交通太拥堵了。

杰克和艾玛很喜欢上学，因为他们能和朋友一起玩儿。另外，他们也喜欢学习。杰克特别喜欢在中午踢足球，而艾玛则喜欢绘画。

放学后，祖母会去校门口接他们，他们简称祖母为"奶奶"。他们走回奶奶家，吃些茶点，然后他们的妈妈会开车来接他们。在奶奶家，他们还可以看会儿电视，或者玩会儿游戏，以作为对他们的奖励。

到家之后，他们全家一起吃晚饭。然后孩子们要完成他们的作业。如果天气好的话，他们还可以和爸爸一起去遛马克斯。

当然，如果他们表现得好，也全部完成作业的话，还可以在睡觉之前玩一会儿电脑游戏。

九点钟之前，杰克和艾玛会换上睡衣、钻进被窝。这时，爸爸妈妈会给他们讲些故事，哄他们睡觉。他俩都喜欢奇幻探险故事，所以可供挑选的好故事有很多。

明天就是周五了，他们开始期待周末的到来。周六上午，爸爸妈妈会带他们去游泳。另外，他们还有很多时间可以做自己喜欢的事情，比如在花园里和马克斯一起踢足球。

Party time!

James Blanshard

Everyone loves going to a party! What all parties have in common is that they are gatherings of friends. They usually have a host, who invites people and organises what happens at the party, and hopefully there is lots of fun.

In the UK there are lots of different kinds of parties. Some types of parties happen on special days of the year when everyone celebrates, and some only happen on very special occasions, like weddings.

Parties on special days of the year include Christmas (December 25), New Year's Eve (December 31), Halloween (October 31), Thanksgiving in the USA (the fourth Thursday in November), and Bonfire Night (November 5) in the UK. Of course, the most common type of party that children have is the birthday parties!

Let's imagine that you're allowed to organise your own birthday party. Here's how you might do it.

First of all, where do you want to have your party? Do you think you'll have it at home, or somewhere else? Some people go out to restaurants or swimming pools to have their party, because there are fun things to do there. If you decide to have your party at home, you'll have to organise food, music and things to do. That could be fun! Let's have the party at home.

Now, shall we have a fancy dress party? For a fancy dress party we'll need to give our friends lots of time to prepare their costumes, and we'll have to tell them what the theme is too. What would you like to dress up as? Good theme ideas might be 'heroes and villains', 'cartoon characters' or 'pirates'. Make sure you send out invitations to your party guests telling them when and where to come.

OK, we need to arrange some games to play. There are lots of traditional games you can prepare. Have you played 'pass the parcel'? You need to wrap up a gift in lots of layers of wrapping or newspaper and get some music ready. When the music begins, you must pass the parcel from person to person in the room, until the music stops. Whoever is holding the parcel when the music stops takes a layer of paper from the parcel. Eventually there won't be any paper left, just the gift! Quizzes for everyone to play are fun too, and 'musical chairs' is a good party game. Make sure you have some good music to play throughout your party.

What are people going to eat and drink? Some fizzy drinks and fruit juice are a good idea. And to eat, how about some sandwiches? Crisps and 'finger food' that you don't need a knife and fork to eat are good for parties, so pizza slices would be great! What about dessert? Jelly and ice cream is a real birthday party favourite!

Now, we'll have to whisper this because it's supposed to be a surprise, but your birthday cake is really important. When dessert has been finished, the lights are suddenly switched off and the cake is brought in, with a glowing candle for every year of your life! Your friends sing the famous 'happy birthday' song and then you blow out the candles and make a wish! The cake is cut so everybody has a slice.

At some point in the party you'll have to open the gifts and cards that your friends have brought for you, and say 'thank you'! A good way to say 'thank you' is to give your friends party bags when they leave. These will have a slice of cake, some sweets, and maybe a little gift too.

Once the party is over, it is time to clean the house! Finally, all that is left to do is put your cards up around your home, and write thank-you notes to your friends for coming to the party!

聚会时间

韩淑俊 译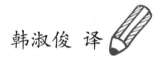

人人都喜欢参加聚会！所有聚会的共同点是朋友们欢聚一堂。聚会通常有一位主办人，负责邀请朋友，安排聚会事宜。如果顺利的话，聚会会非常好玩儿。

在英国，聚会五花八门。有些聚会在一年中的特别日子举行，人人都会参与庆祝；而有些只在特殊场合举行，譬如婚礼。

在一年中可以举行聚会的特别日子包括：圣诞节（12月25日）、新年除夕（12月31日）、万圣夜（10月31日）、美国的感恩节（11月的第四个星期四）和英国的篝火夜（11月5日）。当然，孩子们最常举行的是生日聚会！

假定你获准举办自己的生日聚会，那么你有可能这样来操办：

首先，你想在何处举行聚会？想在家里还是在别的什么地方？有些人在外面的餐厅或者在游泳池举行聚会，因为在那些地方有的可玩儿。如果你决定在家举行，你必须要准备食物和音乐，并安排活动。那会很有趣！那就让我们在家举行一次聚会吧。

那么，我们要不要举行一场化装舞会？要举办化装舞会的话，我们需要给朋友们很多时间去准备服装，还要告诉他们舞会的主题。你想装扮成什么样子呢？主题可以是"英雄和恶棍""卡通人物"或者"海盗"，这些都是不错的点子。你要确保向参加聚会的客人发出邀请，告诉他们聚会的时间和地点。

好了，我们要组织一些游戏来玩儿。有很多传统的游戏可以准备。玩过"传包裹"游戏吗？你需要用很多层包装纸或者报纸包住一份礼物，还要准备播放音乐。当音乐开始时，要将包裹从屋里的一个人传给另一个人，直到音乐停止。当音乐停止时，拿着包裹的人要剥掉一层包装纸。最后，包装纸都没有了，只剩下礼物！组织大家都来玩竞猜游戏也很有趣，还有"抢椅子"也是一种好玩儿的聚会游戏。你要确保在整个聚会中一直有好听的音乐可以播放。

大家来点儿什么吃的喝的呢？喝碳酸饮料和果汁就不错。至于吃的东西，三明治怎么样呢？炸薯片和其他不需要刀叉、用手拿着就能吃的东西都是很不错的聚会食品，所以（聚会时）吃切好的比萨饼就很好！甜点吃什么呢？果冻和冰激凌是生日聚会上人们的最爱！

现在，我们要小声点儿说，因为这应该是一个惊喜，但是你的生日蛋糕真的非常重要。吃完甜点后，灯光突然熄灭，这时有人会把生日蛋糕拿进来，蛋糕上每一支点燃的蜡烛代表着你生命中的一岁。朋友们唱起那首著名的"生日快乐"歌，接着你吹灭蜡烛并许下一个愿望！然后你切开蛋糕，给每人分一块。

在聚会中的某个时候，你将要打开朋友们送给你的礼物和卡片，并说声"谢谢"！对朋友们表示感谢的一个好办法是在他们要离开的时候送给他们聚会礼包，里面装上一块蛋糕、一些糖果，也可以再装一份小礼物。

聚会一结束，就该开始收拾房子了。最后要做的事就是把你收到的卡片摆放在家里，并致信朋友们，感谢他们参加聚会。

Going on holiday

Nancy Dickmann

Most families love to go on holiday together. It is a real treat to leave your ordinary life behind and go somewhere different and exciting! Some families are lucky enough to be able to take more than one holiday a year. If you are ever talking to a British person and you run out of things to say, ask him where he is going on his next holiday—chances are he'll be planning it already!

There are many different types of holidays. Some people enjoy exploring cities, visiting museums and soaking up the atmosphere in cafes. Other people prefer outdoor holidays, where you can hike or go canoeing. Some people like cruises, where the giant ship is like a hotel. Whatever you like to do, there is sure to be a holiday for you!

Beach holidays

Many families go on holiday in the summer, when schools are closed. Beach holidays are very popular in

Britain, and the country has many seaside resorts such as Bournemouth, Blackpool and Brighton. In the past, most British families would have taken their holiday at a British seaside town. However, now many people choose to go abroad instead. One reason for this is to escape the possibility of rain at home! France, Spain and Greece are popular destinations.

On a beach holiday, the main goal is to have fun in the water! Many people enjoy swimming in the sea. If you are more adventurous you might try snorkelling, water-skiing or windsurfing. It's important to wear sun-cream and a hat, otherwise a bad sunburn could spoil your fun! Most holiday resorts also offer indoor activities, such as ping-pong or video arcades.

Road trips

In the United States, summer holidays often involve a road trip. This means packing the whole family into the car and setting out! It is not uncommon to drive hundreds of miles to get to your destination. Some families might head for the beach, but if that is too far then you could go to one of the dozens of national parks. Many people love exploring the natural beauty of places such as Yellowstone or the Grand Canyon.

On a road trip you can stop for lunch at a diner or drive-through restaurant. At night, you might stay at a roadside hotel, called a motel. Or, you could try camping instead! In the summers, campgrounds across the country fill up with people enjoying the outdoor life. Some people stay in tents, and others drive vehicles like a small house on wheels, called RVs. Everyone loves toasting marshmallows and singing songs around a campfire before bed.

Winter holidays

Summer is not the only season for going on holiday. In the winter, many people go skiing. The Alps are a very popular place to ski. The mountain scenery is truly spectacular! If you don't like downhill skiing, at many resorts you can also try cross-country skiing, snowshoeing or tobogganing. After a long day on the slopes it's nice to warm up with a cup of hot chocolate!

Before Christmas, some people take trips to visit Christmas markets. In many European cities, busy outdoor markets will be set up for the month of December. Traders sell food and drink and crafts that can be given as gifts. There are also performances by singers and dancers. These markets are especially popular in Germany.

No matter what kind of holiday you take, there are two things that nearly everyone does. The first is to send postcards to friends and family at home, so they can see a photo of the place where you are! The second is to buy some sort of souvenir to help you remember your trip—maybe a T-shirt or a piece of pottery or art. Then, once you're home it's time to start planning your next holiday!

度 假

韩淑俊 译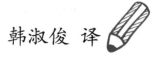

大多数家庭都喜欢一起度假。远离平日的生活，去一个不同的、令人兴奋的地方度假，实属一大乐事！有些家庭很幸运，一年中度假次数不止一次。如果你和一个英国人聊天时觉得没的可聊了，那么就问问他下一个假期打算去哪里 —— 他很可能已经在做计划了！

度假的方式有很多种。有些人喜欢城市观光、参观博物馆或泡在咖啡馆里。有些人则喜欢户外度假，去徒步旅行或划独木舟。还有些人喜欢乘船游览，这类大游船如同酒店一般。不管你喜欢做什么，总有一种度假方式适合你！

海滨假日

很多家庭选择在暑假时外出度假。英国人非常喜欢海滨假日，而英国本土就有很多海滨度假胜地，譬如伯恩茅斯、布莱克浦和布莱顿。过去大多数英国家庭都选择在英国的海滨城镇度假，但是现在有很多人选择出国，其中一个原因是他们想躲避国内随时可能出现的下雨天气。法国、西班牙和希腊都是很受欢迎的目的地。

海滨度假的主要目的是享受水中的乐趣！很多人喜欢在海中游泳。如果你喜欢冒险，可以尝试潜水、滑水或者冲浪。一定要记得擦防晒霜、戴遮阳帽，否则严重的晒伤会扫了你的兴致！大多数度假胜地还提供室内娱乐活动，如乒乓球或电子游戏厅。

驾车旅行

在美国，暑假时人们通常会驾车出行，全家齐上车，一起出发！为到达目的地驱车几百英里是司空见惯的事。有些家庭会去海滨，但是如果去海滨太远的话，你可以从几十个国家公园中选择一个。很多人喜欢去诸如黄石公园或者大峡谷这样的地方领略壮丽的自然风光。

在驾车旅行途中，你可以停下来，在路边的饭馆或者免下车餐馆吃午饭。晚上可以住在叫做汽车旅馆的路边旅馆里。或者你也可以尝试一下露营。在夏季，全国各地的露营地随处可见享受着户外生活的人们。他们有些人住在帐篷里，有些人则驾驶着房车 —— 一种带车轮的房子似的汽车。（露营的）人们都喜欢在睡觉前围着篝火烤棉花糖和唱歌。

冬季假期

夏季并非适宜度假的唯一季节。冬季有很多人去滑雪。阿尔卑斯山是人们非常喜爱的滑雪胜地。那里的山景非常雄伟壮观！如果你不喜欢高山滑雪，也可以在很多旅游胜地尝试越野滑雪、雪地漫步或雪橇滑雪。在雪道上度过了漫长的一天之后，喝杯热巧克力暖和暖和会很惬意。

圣诞节之前，有些人会去圣诞节市场逛逛。欧洲很多城市在 12 月份会搭建许多露天市场，吸引不少人前往。商贩销售食品、饮料和可以作为礼物馈赠的手工艺品。此外还有歌舞表演。这种市场在德国尤其受欢迎。

不管采取哪种方式度假，有两件事几乎是每个人都会做的。一是给朋友和家人寄明信片，让他们看看你所到之地的照片；二是购买某种纪念品，帮助你回忆你的旅行，可以是一件 T 恤衫、一件陶器或者艺术品。然后，等你到家之后，就可以开始为下一个假期制订计划了。

4 Food
饮食

British food

Nancy Dickmann

For many years, British food had a bad reputation around the world. People from other countries thought that British food was all about over-cooked vegetables, tough meat, and bland flavours. They say that French or Italian food has much more to offer. In the past, this might have been true. But is it still the case? Most people would say that it is not! In Britain there are more than one hundred restaurants that have earned a Michelin Star, the highest honour for fine food. Waves of immigrants from around the world have meant that you can find any type of food in Britain, from Indian and Polish to Ethiopian and Brazilian. So what exactly is British food these days?

Traditional favourites

Although food in Britain has become much more cosmopolitan over the last few decades, many traditional dishes are still favourites. Fish and chips is probably one of the most famous. It includes a fillet of white fish, usually cod or haddock, that is battered and deep-fried. The fish is served with thick French fries, called 'chips' in Britain. This dish is served in restaurants and pubs, but can also be bought from traditional 'chippies' in every town.

Cottage pie is another traditional favourite. There are many variations, but the dish always includes minced beef baked with a topping of mashed potato. If it is made using minced lamb instead, then the dish is often called 'shepherd's pie'. Lancashire hotpot is another filling traditional dish. It consists of meat (usually lamb or mutton) and vegetables, topped with sliced potatoes and cooked for hours in a heavy dish. Cornish pasties are a popular snack that originally came from the southwest of the country, but which can now be found everywhere. They are made from a mix of meat and vegetables folded into a pastry crust. Pasties were originally developed as a filling lunch for tin miners who worked deep underground. Now you can find pasties with all sorts of fillings, from turkey and stuffing to chocolate and banana!

Drinks

No discussion of British food would be complete without a mention of their two most famous drinks, tea and beer. Tea has been popular in Britain since the 17th century, and most often means black tea. Many people add milk or lemon, and some add sugar as well. Stopping for a tea break is a time-honoured British custom, although these days some people drink coffee instead! Local brewers all over the country brew their own varieties of beer. Although continental lagers have become popular, many people still prefer the traditional beers such as ale, stout and bitter. Beer is normally served by the pint, so if someone asks you, "Fancy a pint?" then they are offering you a beer!

British or not?

Over the last few decades, the issue of what exactly British food is has become more complicated. Immigrants from other countries have brought their own food traditions, and in many cases these have mixed with British dishes to create a new type of cuisine. One example is 'curry', a general term for Indian food. Although originally treated with suspicion, curry has become so popular that many people see it as quintessentially British. New dishes have been invented in Britain, such as chicken tikka masala, which is one of the most popular dishes in the country. Another example of Indian and British food mixing is the availability of chips served with curry sauce! Italian dishes such as pizza and pasta have become very popular, especially spaghetti bolognese. Many of these dishes are given a uniquely British 'twist', for example, putting baked beans—or even chicken tikka masala—on a pizza!

英国饮食

张华嵩 译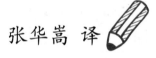

  多年来，英国食物在全世界的口碑一直不佳。外国人一度认为，英国食物就意味着煮得过火的蔬菜、烤得太老的肉和平淡的口味，而法国菜和意大利菜则品种丰富得多。过去可能的确如此，那么如今呢？多数人会说，事实并非如此。英国已有逾百家的饭馆被评为"米其林星级餐厅"，这可是美食界的最高荣誉。来自世界各地一波又一波的移民意味着，在英国你能品尝到各国美食，无论是印度、波兰还是埃塞俄比亚或巴西风味，应有尽有。那么今天的"英国美食"究竟有哪些呢？

传统美食依然得宠

尽管过去几十年里英国的食物已经变得非常国际化，但许多传统菜肴依然得宠，其中知名度最高的食品之一可能要数炸鱼薯条了。炸鱼薯条包括去骨白鱼片与粗粗的炸薯条（French fries，在英国称为 chips），鱼肉通常是鳕鱼或黑线鳕鱼，将其裹上面糊煎炸而成。炸鱼薯条在饭馆或是酒吧都有出售，在遍布各城镇的传统薯条店也能买到。

农家馅饼也是受青睐的传统美食，其做法多样，但必不可少的是将牛肉馅以土豆泥覆盖后加以烘烤。如果选用羔羊肉馅，这种馅饼则被称为"牧羊人馅饼"。另一道让人胃口大开的传统菜肴是兰开夏郡火锅，里面有肉（通常是羔羊肉或羊肉）和蔬菜，上面盖着土豆片，在厚实的容器中经数小时炖制而成。康沃尔菜肉烘饼是一种受欢迎的小吃，它源于英国西南部，现在已是随处可见了。它是将肉和蔬菜混合，卷进一张面饼而制成的。这一食物起初是在地下深处工作的锡矿工人拿来充饥的午餐，如今，你能吃到各种馅料的康沃尔菜肉烘饼，有火鸡和填料馅儿的，还有巧克力和香蕉馅儿的。

饮品

谈到英国食物，人们定会提到两种最有名的饮品：茶和啤酒。自 17 世纪以来，茶在英国风行至今，而在这里，茶通常指的是红茶。很多人在茶里加奶或柠檬，也有人加糖。尽管今天有些英国人已改喝咖啡了，但"停下手边工作享受茶歇时光"仍是由来已久的英国传统。英国各地的啤酒酿造者酿制的啤酒可谓品种多样。尽管欧陆淡啤酒很是流行，很多人依然钟爱传统啤酒，如麦芽啤、黑啤和苦啤酒。啤酒一般以品脱为单位，因此若有人问你："想来一品脱么？"那就是要请你喝啤酒啦！

究竟是不是英国食物？

几十年来，"到底什么是英国食物"这一问题已变得越来越复杂。外来的移民带来了自己的饮食传统，它们大多已与英国菜相互交融并形成了新的菜式，咖喱就是其中一例。咖喱是对印度食物的统称。想当初英国人还对咖喱心存怀疑，现如今它却大受欢迎，很多人都已经把它看作是典型的英国食物了。新菜式不断被推出，如印式烤鸡，这可谓是英国最受欢迎的食物之一。另一个英印菜肴融合的例子就是将炸薯条佐以咖喱酱来食用。比萨和意大利面等意大利食物也很流行，尤其是意大利式杂酱面。其中很多菜式已经过了独特的英式"处理"，例如把烘豆甚至是印式烤鸡作为比萨顶料！

American food

Nancy Dickmann

American food is famous throughout the world. Thanks to fast food restaurants such as McDonald's, the typical American meal of hamburger, French fries and Coca-Cola or a milkshake can be eaten in more than 100 countries around the world. Other American foods such as barbecued pork ribs, apple pie and hot dogs are also well-known. But is there more to American food?

The melting pot

America is a nation of immigrants, and its citizens come from all over the world. Because of this, there is a huge variety of food on offer! Most cities will have restaurants offering French, Italian, Chinese, Indian, Thai, Mexican, Polish and Spanish food, as well as much more. You can find just about anything you like to eat in a big city. Many of these international cooking styles have been adapted to become uniquely American.

Some food from immigrant groups has become popular throughout the country. Millions of Jewish people, mainly from Eastern Europe, came to the United States in the 19th and 20th centuries, and they brought dishes such as bagels (a round bread roll with a hole in the middle), lox (cured salmon), borscht (a rich soup made from beetroot), latkes (pancakes made from grated potatoes), and pastrami (a type of sliced meat).

Immigrants from Italy brought dishes such as pizza and pasta. Pizza is now one of the most popular foods in the country! Each region has its own style of pizza, such as New York, Chicago deep dish, St. Louis or California styles. Most pizza has tomato sauce and cheese on top of a flat bread crust, but additional toppings can be anything from sausage to mushrooms to pineapple!

In the last few decades, Mexicans have been one of the biggest immigrant groups, and you can now find Mexican food almost anywhere you go. Most dishes are based around meat (usually chicken, beef or pork) marinated in chilli peppers and spices, cooked with vegetables and served with cheese and flatbread. Popular dishes include enchiladas, tacos, burritos and fajitas. Nachos, a snack made from crispy fried corn tortillas covered in chillies and cheese, are served at many sports events and snack bars.

Regional foods

The different regions of the United States often have their own specialty food. New England, in the northeast of the country, is famous for clam chowder, a thick fish stew. In the southeast, you will come across a type of cooking known as 'soul food'. This style was developed by the African slaves who once worked on farms here. Because they were poor, they often cooked with unpopular cuts of meat and used plants that were easy to grow. In Louisiana, the local specialty is 'cajun' food. This is an unlikely mix of French, African and Native American traditions, and it is often very spicy!

If you head for the southwestern part of the country, you will find 'Tex-Mex' cooking. This style is similar to Mexican food, but with an American twist. One of the most famous Tex-Mex dishes is chilli con carne, usually just called 'chilli'. This thick stew is made from ground beef, beans, tomatoes and a lot of chilli peppers. There are contests to see who can cook the spiciest chilli! California is known for food using healthy ingredients such as avocado and bean sprouts, and also of 'fusion cuisine', a type of cooking that uses fresh, local ingredients and combines them in unexpected ways.

There are times of the year when people from all regions eat the same food. Thanksgiving is celebrated in late November, and families gather to share the traditional meal of roast turkey, served with cranberry sauce, mashed potatoes and cornbread. Don't forget the pumpkin pie for dessert!

美国饮食

张华嵩　译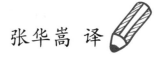

美国的饮食可谓世界闻名。由于麦当劳这样的快餐店，全世界一百多个国家都可享用到典型的美国食物，如汉堡、炸薯条、可口可乐或奶昔。其他美国食物，如烤猪排、苹果派和热狗也很出名。那么，除此以外呢？

大熔炉

美国是一个移民国家，其公民来自世界各地。因此，在这里可以品尝到各式各样的食物。大多数城市都拥有各式风味的餐厅，有法国、意大利、中国、印度、泰国、墨西哥、波兰、西班牙和其他多种风味的美食供人们尽情享用。若是身处大城市，无论你想吃什么，都能得到满足。这些异国烹饪方式中的很多种在经过改良后已经变得具有美国特色了。

一些随移民进入美国的食物已风靡全国。在19世纪和20世纪，数百万主要来自东欧的犹太人来到美国，带来了百吉圈（一种中间有孔的圆面包卷）、熏鲑鱼、罗宋汤（一种甜菜做的浓汤）、土豆烙饼（擦碎的马铃薯制成的薄煎饼）和五香熏牛肉（将牛肉切片制成）等佳肴。

意大利移民带来了比萨、意大利面等美食，如今比萨已是美国最受欢迎的食物之一。说起比萨，可谓一个地区一个样儿，有纽约式、芝加哥深盘式、圣路易斯式和加利福尼亚式等。大多数比萨都有一层面包饼皮，上面浇着番茄酱和奶酪，其他的配料可以是香肠、蘑菇和菠萝等任何食物。

在最近几十年，墨西哥人已成为美国最大的移民团体之一，如今几乎走到哪里都能看到墨西哥食物。多数墨西哥菜肴以辣椒和香料腌制的肉类（通常是鸡肉、牛肉或猪肉）为主料，与蔬菜一起烹制，佐以奶酪和面饼食用。受欢迎的菜肴包括辣椒肉馅玉米卷饼、墨西哥煎玉米卷、玉米面卷饼和珐西塔。烤干酪辣味玉米片——一种覆着辣椒和奶酪、口感酥脆的炸玉米片制成的零食，是很多体育比赛场地和小吃店的常见食物。

地方食物

美国的不同地区通常都有独具地区特色的食物。东北部的新英格兰地区以蛤蜊浓汤著名，这是一种蛤蜊炖制的浓汤。在东南部，你能品尝到一种被称为"非裔美国人大餐"的菜系，这一菜系由曾在这里的农场上劳作的非洲奴隶创立。由于贫穷，他们常用下脚料中的碎肉和易于种植的蔬菜烹制食物。在路易斯安那，当地的特色菜肴叫做"卡金菜"，由法国、非洲和印第安传统菜式以不可思议的方式混合而成，味道常常十分辛辣。

如果去美国西南部，你会见识到"墨式德州"烹饪。它与墨西哥食物很相似，只是已被美国人加以改造。最知名的墨式德州菜肴之一是香辣肉酱，通常简称为"辣子"。这道香浓的炖菜由碎牛肉、豆子、西红柿和大量辣椒烹制而成。人们还会组织看谁做的"辣子"最辣的比赛！加利福尼亚出名的是由牛油果和豆芽这类健康食材烹制而成的食物，这里有名的还有"混合菜式"，它取材于本地的新鲜原料，经巧妙搭配烹制而成。

一年中也有几次，无论身在美国何地，人们会吃同样的食物。11月底，人们会庆祝感恩节，家人团聚，共享配以越橘酱、土豆泥和玉米面包的烤火鸡传统大餐。可别忘了还有南瓜饼当甜点！

Breakfast time

James Blanshard

There's a saying in the UK and US that 'breakfast is the most important meal of the day', and for lots of people in the West, this is definitely true!

The 'full English' breakfast is famous around the world. It's a very filling meal, but not a very healthy one if you eat it every day. Bacon and eggs are always included, and then all sorts of other fried foods are added. This could include sausages, tomatoes, mushrooms, hash browns (potato patties) or fried bread. In some parts of the UK, black pudding is included in a full English breakfast. Black pudding sounds like a dessert, but in fact it is dried blood mixed up with fat or another thickener, rolled into a big sausage!

The full English breakfast is popular, but in fact British people eat all sorts of things when they wake up in the morning. Cooking up bacon, eggs and sausages can take a long while, and most people don't have enough time to do that every day. It leaves behind lots of greasy washing-up to do too. Yuk!

In fact, the most popular breakfast foods in the UK are breakfast cereals, like cornflakes, which were invented in America over 100 years ago. There is a big selection of breakfast cereals. These are usually made from corn, wheat, rice or oats, and are eaten in a bowl with cold milk.

When the weather gets chilly though, a lot of people in the US and UK like to eat hot cereals. Have you ever tried porridge? Porridge is a mixture of oats and hot milk or water, usually with something added to sweeten it, like honey or syrup. In the US, porridge is called oatmeal. A similar hot breakfast that is popular in the southern states of the US is grits. Grits are a cereal made from maize. Like porridge, grits are gloopy and sticky. They are often topped with gravy or butter.

Because the US has so many different cultures, there are lots of different popular breakfasts. A favourite breakfast treat in America is waffles or pancakes, with maple syrup. Maple syrup is made from the sap of the maple tree, and it is mostly made in Canada and Vermont, the US, where maple trees grow well.

Bagels are also popular as breakfast meals in the US and UK. They are doughy rings of bread that are tasty with cream cheese. You can toast bagels and eat them with all sorts of fillings, like salmon and scrambled eggs. Yum!

When the weather is warmer, many people in the UK and America like to eat a 'continental breakfast'. This is a lighter breakfast that is often eaten in the warmer countries of Europe, like France and Italy. A continental breakfast might have a sweet pastry, some yoghurt and some fruit.

And finally, very importantly, most adults in the West won't feel like they have eaten their breakfast unless they have drunk a hot drink with it. In the UK, tea is the most popular drink, though some people prefer coffee. In America tea isn't drunk so much, so coffee is definitely the more popular choice. Children might drink milk or fruit juice with breakfast.

But is breakfast really the most important meal of the day? Scientists seem to think so. Research suggests that when we eat breakfast in the morning, it gives us energy and helps to keep our bodies healthy. So whether you eat bacon and eggs, pastries, porridge or pancakes, don't forget to eat your breakfast!

早餐时间

张艳波 译

英美有句名言："早餐是一天中最重要的一餐。"对许多西方人而言，的确如此！

"英式早餐"在世界上享有盛名。这种早餐会让人吃得很饱，但假如你每天都享用的话就不利于健康了。英式早餐总有熏肉和煎蛋，再加上其他各种煎炸食物，可能是香肠、番茄、蘑菇、土豆煎饼（马铃薯馅饼）或烤面包片。英国有些地方的英式早餐还包括血肠。血肠乍听起来像是甜点，但实际上是干血加上油脂或其他增稠剂卷成的大香肠。

英式早餐很受欢迎，但实际上英国人的早餐是各式各样的。烹制熏肉、鸡蛋和香肠太费时间，多数人没有充足的时间每天都做这种早餐，更何况吃完之后还要洗一大堆油腻的餐具，太讨厌啦！

实际上，英国最受欢迎的早餐是谷类食品，如一百多年前源自美国的玉米片。可供选择的谷类食品很多，通常由玉米、小麦、稻米或燕麦制成，用冷牛奶冲到碗里食用。

然而天气转冷的时候，许多英美人喜欢吃加热的谷类粥。你吃过麦片粥吗？麦片粥由燕麦和热牛奶或水混合而成，通常还配以蜂蜜或糖浆等甜料。在美国，麦片粥叫做燕麦粥。美国南方流行一种类似的热早餐叫玉米粥，由玉米粉做成。玉米粥像麦片粥一样又浓又黏，上面经常会加上肉卤或奶油。

美国文化丰富多彩，流行的早餐也是花样繁多。最受欢迎的早餐之一是抹上枫糖浆的华夫饼或薄煎饼。枫糖浆由枫树的汁液制成，主要产地是盛产枫树的加拿大和美国佛蒙特州。

在英美两国，百吉圈也是颇受欢迎的早餐食品，松软的面包圈佐以奶油干酪，十分可口。你也可以烤制百吉圈，再配上各种夹馅，如鲑鱼和炒鸡蛋，太美味啦！

天气转暖时，很多英美人喜欢吃欧式早餐。这种早餐比较清淡，通常流行于比较温暖的欧洲国家，像法国和意大利。欧式早餐一般包括甜饼、酸奶和水果。

最后，非常重要的一点是，西方多数成年人总觉得早餐必须有热饮喝才算是真正的早餐。在英国，尽管有些人更喜欢喝咖啡，但茶才是最受欢迎的早餐饮料。美国人喝茶不多，咖啡绝对是更受欢迎的饮料。孩子们早餐时一般喝牛奶或果汁。

但是早餐真的是一天中最重要的一餐吗？科学家们似乎这样认为。研究表明，早餐能使我们精力充沛、身体健康。因此，不管你是吃熏肉加鸡蛋、糕饼、麦片粥还是薄煎饼，可别忘了吃早餐哦！

Food and marriage

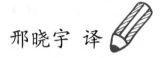

邢晓宇 译

On our first date, my Scottish husband told me how much he loved Chinese food. Seeing his face filled with excitement and a desire to please me, I, a self-proclaimed good cook, couldn't help wondering to myself, "Who has told him about my cooking skills?"

The first time he invited me out for dinner, he chose a Chinese restaurant called Taiyuan Restaurant. As soon as we sat down, he eagerly picked up the menu and said to me with a broad smile, "Chicken Curry and Beef with Black Bean Sauce are my favourites!" Watching him ravenously devouring the Chinese food that was totally localised and nothing like the real thing, I felt sorry for him from the bottom of my heart.

In the days that followed, I was determined to cook as many wonderful meals for him as I could and let him experience real Chinese cuisine. However, it didn't turn out as I hoped. No matter how hard I tried to cook Chinese food and no matter how much time I spent on it, there was always anticipation and then disappointment written on his face. If it were not for his handsome face, I would have stormed out of the door. This not only dampened my enthusiasm, it also shook my confidence in my ability to cook good food. Sometimes I gave away some of my specialities such as Stewed Fish in Brown Sauce, Stewed Chicken with Chestnuts, Yu-Shiang Aubergines and Spare Ribs with Taro to my Chinese friends so that I could regain some confidence from their admiration. In the first two years of our marriage, this conversation could often be heard in our home, "Why can't you cook good Chicken Curry like a proper Chinese chef does?" and my reply, "We Chinese don't eat curry, nor do we want to eat your tasteless chicken breast every day!"

The simple Western-style diet, particularly the British style, had a deep-rooted influence on my husband. In his mind, chicken and beef were the best food, and the only seafood he could eat was prawn and a few kinds of fish. Deep-fried was the way he liked to cook fish. What annoyed him was that I hated deep-fried food. Every time he smiled and praised his Aberdeen-Angus beef roast saying how tasty it was, I would hold up a big sea crab, chew heartily and ignore him. Here in Scotland a big sea crab cost just around £2. As no one else seemed to like it, I made the most of that.

I would never forget the expression on the face of my 195-centimetre-tall Scottish husband when he first saw the huge pigs' heads in the fridge of a Chinese supermarket. It was a mixture of shock, confusion and some panic. While I was excited about buying a big pig's head for only £1.50, he whispered quietly, "If you want to take that head home, please go home by train. (I'll take the car by myself.)"

The first time I took him to my parents' home, on the plane I was racking my brains for some ideas on what foods I could get him to try. After all, his palate had been ruined by years of junk food. My intention was to broaden his culinary horizons and hopefully help him to appreciate good food.

My dad and mum picked Quanjude Peking Roast Duck for the welcoming dinner. To my surprise, he seemed to really enjoy roast duck. He ate the meat with relish and cleaned his plate, but then refused to touch the best part, the crisp skin. Mum got anxious and said to him in Chinese, "John, try this. It tastes great." I responded, "Mum, never mind. It's better that he doesn't eat it; then nobody fights with me over it." The incredible thing was that he understood our conversation! He picked up a piece of skin, put it on a thin pancake and chewed it with a look of wonder on his face, and then ate the rest with a big smile. After that, Dad asked me, "Now do you believe that he and your mother spoke for five minutes on the phone? Your mum spoke Chinese and John English, but their questions and answers really corresponded. It was like magic."

I must say that training my husband in good cuisine on our trip to China was worthwhile because he tried crab, jellyfish and deep-fried silkworm chrysalis for the first time. Back home he told his friends that the jellyfish tasted like rubber, though.

Cooking and eating has been a part of our everyday married life. I enjoy the Scottish breakfast that my husband brings to my bedside every Saturday, and he has started to accept the Chinese stir-fried noodles and fried dumplings I make. However, he often teases me with these words, "Having travelled through most of China, I can say that the most delicious Chinese chicken curry is to be found right here in Scotland!" What can I say?!

饮食与婚姻

言枫 文

第一次约会，苏格兰老公就不无夸张地对我讲他是如何如何地喜爱中国饭。看着他脸上那副兴奋与讨好的神情，自诩厨艺颇佳的我暗地里咬牙：是不是哪个多嘴的告诉了他我的做饭手艺？

第一次请我出去吃饭，老公选的是一家名叫"太原小馆"的中餐厅。坐下后，他迫不及待地捧起菜单，满脸堆笑地对我说："咖喱鸡和豉汁牛肉是我的最爱！"看着他狼吞虎咽地吃着那些已经本地化的实在不敢恭维的中餐，心底不由得可怜起这个家伙来。

以后的日子里，我就做好了调理他肠胃的准备，想让他领教一下什么是我中华泱泱大国的饮食文化。可是事与愿违，无论我怎样费时费力变着花样地做一些真正的中餐，先是盼望后是失望的表情总是重复出现在他的脸上。如果不是他那张脸确实有些英俊的话，我恨不得摔门而去。这不仅仅影响到我的心情，更打击了我的自信。有的时候我不得不把做好的红烧鱼、栗子鸡、鱼香茄子、香芋排骨等送给中国朋友，以便在他们的赞叹声中找回些面子。婚后的两年里，在我们家经常会听到这样的对话："为什么你是中国人却做不好咖喱鸡？""我们不吃咖喱，我们也不爱天天吃无味的鸡胸！"

西式尤其是英式饮食结构的简单化，已经对老公造成了根深蒂固的影响。在他的概念里鸡肉、牛肉是最好的东西，而他能接受的所谓的海鲜也不过就是虾和二三种鱼而已。鱼的做法也永远只是油炸。让他恼火的是我对此总是嗤之以鼻，当他摇头晃脑地赞叹阿伯丁牛排是如何的美味的时候，我手里正举着一个大海蟹大嚼特嚼，并回以满脸的不屑。这里的大海蟹只要 2 英镑左右就可以买到一个，我可要大快朵颐。

我永远不会忘记这个身高一米九多的苏格兰大男人，在中国超市里看到摆在冷柜里的猪头时的表情：夹杂着震惊与困惑还有些许恐惧。当我为只花 1.5 英镑就可以买一个大猪头兴奋的时候，耳边响起的是他亲切的低语："如果你想把这个头带回家的话，请你坐火车好吗？"

结婚后头一次带他回娘家，在飞机上想了一路：在他吃了那么多年的垃圾之后，怎么带他去吃一些好东西？其实真正的目的是让这个乡下人开开眼界，也好在以后的日子里有所改变。

老爸老妈的接风宴设在全聚德。让我吃惊的是，老公对烤鸭情有独钟。风卷残云般地猛往嘴里塞，但是对最好吃的鸭皮却碰也不碰。老妈急了，用中文对他讲："John，你吃这个，这个可好吃了！"我说："妈你别管他，他不吃正好没人跟我抢。"他却鬼使神差般地听懂了，夹起一小块放进饼里，先尝了尝，然后就开始面带微笑地将大半盘全都消灭了。老爸问我："现在你信你妈跟他在电话里聊了 5 分钟的事了吧？他俩一个说中文，一个说英文，问的和答的都很正确，神了！"

回国的培训还是小有成效的，老公生平第一次吃了大闸蟹，吃了海蜇，甚至吃了炸蚕蛹，虽然后来他对他的朋友们说海蜇吃起来像胶皮。

　　婚后的生活就这样在每日做饭、吃饭中一天天走过来的，我快乐地享受着每个星期六老公端到床头的苏格兰式早餐，老公也开始慢慢接受我做的中式炒面和油煎饺子。老公常挂在嘴边故意找茬儿的话就是："走了大半个中国，最好的中式咖喱鸡在苏格兰。"唉！孺子难教也！

5 Clothing
服饰

School uniforms

James Blanshard

School uniforms are common in the UK and US, but not all schools have them. They are usually formal clothes that all boys and girls must wear at their school, and they will have the school badge or motto so they can be easily identified.

The colour of the uniform varies from school to school. Common colours are blue or grey, but it could be any smart dark colour, like very dark red or green.

For boys, most school uniforms will consist of a shirt and trousers, usually with shoes, although some schools allow dark trainers. Ties are common too. These will often be striped in the school's colours. Some schools have a blazer jacket, which is good for keeping warm in the winter months. Luckily, most schools don't insist that the children wear their blazers in the warmer summer months too!

Girls will often wear a blazer, like the boys, a pleated skirt and a blouse, along with smart shoes.

Sometimes, younger children and older children at the same school have different uniforms. They will usually wear the same colours, but it could be that older girls are allowed to wear trousers, or that boys don't have to wear blazers when they are older. This is another way for teachers to identify their students, and it also helps the teenage students as they grow up.

School uniforms can vary depending on the type of school too. Some of the older, more traditional private schools in the UK and USA insist on uniforms that have been worn at the school for many years. These are usually very formal. If you ever get the chance to visit a city like Oxford in the UK, where there are many private schools, take a good look at what the children are wearing. You might be surprised! For example, some children have to wear special hats as part of their uniform. Boys may have soft caps in the school's colours, and girls will sometimes have formal straw hats.

Do you think school uniforms are a good thing? Lots of teachers think so. They often help teachers to tell which students are from their school, and they help children and parents because they don't have to worry about what to wear every day.

Some people think that having a school uniform makes children work harder. They think it prevents bullying because children feel more fellowship with one another.

It can also give children a sense of pride in their school. Some schools take great pride in their uniform and the smartness of their students, but not all students like to wear the uniform!

Some students will try to bend the school rules and wear bright shoes, or customise their clothes so they don't look like everyone else. Bending the rules sometimes ends up with students getting into trouble with the teachers or their parents. To try to stop this, some schools give their students the chance to vote to decide what they want their uniform to be!

Other schools have decided that going to school should be completely free, and so many schools don't have a uniform because it costs money to buy.

What do you think? Are school uniforms a good idea?

Did you know: The very first school uniforms were worn in England 500 years ago when Henry VIII was the king of England! The main thing that was worn then was a blue coat, because blue was the least expensive dye for colouring the clothes. The schools at the time were religious, so the blue coats were a sign of humility for the pupils.

校　服

张华嵩　译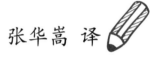

　　校服在英美两国很普遍，但并非所有学校都有校服。校服通常指的是所有男生和女生在校期间必须穿着的正装，其上面的校徽或校训使得他们一眼就能被认出。

　　校服的颜色因校而异。常见的颜色是蓝色和灰色，但也可能是其他漂亮的暗色，如暗红和深绿。

　　男生的校服大多包括衬衣和长裤，通常还搭配专门的鞋子，也有学校允许学生穿深色运动鞋。校服往往配有领带，领带条纹通常是学校的标志颜色。有的学校出于冬天保暖的考虑，会为学生准备轻便夹克衫。所幸的是，大多数学校并不强制学生在炎炎夏日里穿着这些夹克衫。

女生往往也会像男生一样穿着夹克衫，另外还有百褶裙和女装衬衫，并搭配有漂亮的鞋子。

有时同校而不同年龄的学生，校服也有所不同。这些校服颜色通常相同，但有时高年级女生可以穿长裤，或是高年级男生可以不穿夹克衫。这样有利于老师辨认学生，同时对成长中的青春期学生也是有好处的。

校服样式也会因学校类型的差异而有所不同。英美国家一些历史悠久、比较传统的私立学校把穿着多年的校服作为传统保留，这些学校的校服通常非常正式。如果你有机会来到诸如英国牛津这样拥有很多私立学校的城市，一定要好好看看学生们穿着的校服。你也许会感到很惊讶！比如：一些孩子必须戴一顶特殊的帽子，因为帽子也是校服的一部分。男生可能要戴与校服同色的软帽，女生有时要戴很正式的草帽。

你觉得穿着校服是件好事儿吗？很多教师都这样认为，因为校服能够帮助他们辨认出本校的学生，而学生和他们的家长则不用再为每天穿什么衣服上学而费心。

有人认为，穿校服可以使学生学习更用功。一样的穿着可以加深学生对彼此的认同感，从而避免恃强凌弱事件的发生。

同时，校服还能给予学生一种身为学校一份子的荣誉感。而校服和学生身着校服时的精神劲儿更是让一些学校引以为荣。但是，可不是所有学生都爱穿校服！

一些学生为了显得与众不同，会故意不按校规着装，穿着亮色的鞋子或是修改校服。这样做的后果是有时会让学生在老师或家长那里惹上麻烦。为了避免这一情况，有些学校给予学生权利，让他们投票决定校服的设计方案！

还有一些学校认为学校教育应当是完全免费的。因此很多学校没有校服，因为它们需要花钱购买。

那么你的态度呢——上学穿校服是个好主意么？

你是否知道：最早的校服诞生于500年前亨利八世执政期间的英国。当时校服的主体是一件蓝色的外套，因为蓝色染料当时最便宜。同时由于当时英国的学校是教会学校，学生身着蓝色校服表达了一种谦卑的态度。

History of clothes

James and Kate Blanshard

What do you think British people wear? If you come to Britain expecting to see a businessman in a bowler hat, you will be disappointed! Although men used to wear bowler hats, it is very unusual to see anyone in a formal hat today. Clothes that are common in Britain now are suits, T-shirts and jeans, but they have not always been worn there. Clothes and fashions have changed a lot in Britain's history.

Early clothes in Britain were made of furs, animal skins or wool because they are warm materials. In the 1500s wealthy people began to wear silks and cottons. Women wore frames of whale bone or wood under their dresses! A wealthy woman of that time would wear a large wig, hold a folding fan and have a large hooped petticoat under her dress. She would also paint her face white, and might paint a small black dot to cover up a spot.

By the 1800s, outfits were different. Men often wore a waistcoat, jacket and trousers, known as a three-piece suit, which is still worn on smart occasions today. This looked very different from the three-cornered hats and long, formal frock coats they had worn before. In the early 1900s, clothes gradually changed to become more practical, and it became acceptable for women to wear trousers.

Scotland and Wales both have a national dress. In Scotland it is traditional for men to wear a kilt. The pattern on the kilt will be a type of tartan, which is a series of thin overlapping stripes in different colours. The large Scottish families have their own special tartans.

Welsh traditional dress for women and girls was developed in the 1800s. The costume consists of a long black wool skirt with a white apron, a long sleeved white blouse covered with a red wool shawl, and a tall black hat with a wide brim tied under the chin with a big white bow.

England does not have a recognised national dress, although there are some famous traditional costumes. Outside Buckingham Palace in London there are royal foot guards on duty. They each wear a very smart red tunic with a high collar and shiny gold buttons, with black trousers and strong black boots for marching in. However, the most impressive part of their uniform is their very tall, furry black hat with a gold strap, which is made of bearskin and comes very low over the guard's eyes. These strange looking hats were first worn by British soldiers in 1814 to make them look taller and scarier to their enemies!

Another famous uniform is worn by the British police force. This is navy blue all over. Some policemen still wear a tall, bell-shaped hard hat, which they originally used to stand on to see or climb over walls! It makes them easy to find in crowds too.

Since the 1300s, court judges have worn fur and silk-lined robes. In those times, different coloured robes were worn in different seasons, for example, green in summer, purple in winter and red for special occasions. Today, most judges wear red or black robes. Judges and lawyers only started wearing wigs in the late 1600s, when it was fashionable, and they have done so ever since. Some judges' wigs are very long, and can cost over £1000! However, judges in most of the courts are now no longer required to wear wigs.

What other unusual British costumes are there? Another type of old English costume is worn by Morris dancers, who are traditional English country dancers. They often wear long white socks with ribbons crossed over their shirts and maybe a black or straw hat. They also often wear bells on their shoes that ring when they dance and they play traditional musical instruments like drums and whistles.

In east London a tradition grew up in the 1800s of important street sellers wearing pearl buttons on their hats. Soon they were wearing shiny buttons all over and they became known as Pearly Kings and Pearly Queens. Modern-day Pearly Kings and Queens collect money for charities and can still be seen in these traditional clothes today!

服饰的历史

韩淑俊 译

　　你认为英国人的穿戴会是什么样的？如果你到英国想看到一个戴着圆顶硬礼帽的商人，那你会感到失望。虽然英国男人过去经常戴圆顶硬礼帽，但是现在戴这种正式帽子的人已非常罕见。现在英国人通常穿西服、T 恤衫和牛仔裤，但人们并不是一开始就这样穿的。英国历史上，服饰和时尚已经历多次变化。

　　英国早期的服饰由毛皮、兽皮或者羊毛制成，因为这些材料都能保暖。16 世纪时，富人开始穿戴丝织品和棉制品。女人衣服的内衬由鲸骨或木头作框架。

那时富有的女人经常头戴大假发，手拿折叠扇，身穿内衬巨大裙撑的服装。她们还会把脸搽成白色，并可能画一个小黑点以遮盖斑点。

到 19 世纪，人们的装束已有所不同。男人们经常穿马甲、短上衣和裤子，即所谓的三件套。如今，人们在讲究的场合还会穿这种服装。三件套看起来和人们以前穿戴的三角帽及正式的长礼服大衣截然不同。20 世纪早期，服饰渐渐变得更加实用，女人穿裤子被人们所接受了。

苏格兰和威尔士都有民族服装。在苏格兰，男人有穿苏格兰短裙的传统。苏格兰短裙上的格子图案由一系列不同颜色相互重叠的细条纹构成。苏格兰的大家族都有自己独特的格子图案。

威尔士女子的传统服饰是在 19 世纪形成的，这种服饰包括配有白色围裙的黑色羊毛长裙，搭配红色羊毛披肩的白色长袖衬衫和黑色宽檐高帽，帽子通常带有一条宽大的白色系带，在下巴下方打成蝴蝶结。

虽然英格兰有一些著名的传统服饰，但是却没有公认的民族服饰。伦敦白金汉宫外面有皇家步兵近卫军值勤。他们都穿着帅气的红色高领短上衣，饰以闪亮的金色纽扣，配以黑色长裤和用以行进的结实黑靴。但是他们的制服令人印象最深刻的是带有金黄色带子的黑色高筒毛帽子。帽子由熊皮制成，戴得非常低，几近士兵眼睛的上部。1814 年，英国士兵首次戴上这种造型奇怪的帽子，这使他们显得更高大，更能威慑敌人。

另一种颇为有名的服装是英国警察穿的制服。制服全身为深蓝色。有些警察还戴着高高的钟形硬帽，而这种帽子最初是供警察站在上面张望或翻墙的。这种帽子也使他们在人群中非常抢眼。

　　自14世纪以来，法官在法庭上就开始穿外面是皮毛、衬里是丝绸的长袍。那时，法官在不同季节穿不同颜色的袍子，譬如：夏季穿绿色，冬季穿紫色，在特殊场合穿红色。现在，大多数法官穿红色或者黑色的法袍。法官和律师从17世纪后期才开始戴假发，那时假发非常流行，从那以后他们一直如此穿戴。有些法官的假发很长，可能价值1000多英镑。但是，今天大多数法庭上的法官已不再被要求戴假发了。

　　英国还有其他特别的服饰吗？另外一种古老的服装是英国传统乡村舞演员 —— 莫里斯舞蹈演员们穿的服装。他们通常穿着白色长袜，衬衫外面扎着彩带，有时还戴一顶黑帽或草帽。他们还经常穿着带铃铛的鞋子，跳舞时铃铛会随之响起。他们演奏传统的乐器，譬如鼓和小竖笛。

　　19世纪，伦敦东部开始兴起一项传统，一些有影响力的街头小贩开始戴缀有珍珠纽扣的帽子。很快他们开始穿缀满闪亮纽扣的衣服，并以"珠母纽王"和"珠母纽女王"的名字为人们所知。现在，"珠母纽王"和"珠母纽女王"为慈善机构筹集善款，仍然会身着这种传统的服饰出现。

The Scottish kilt

Kenneth and Joan Cameron

It is said, probably as a joke, that when a band of Scottish soldiers marched through a French village, the villagers looked at each other in surprise and one said:

"What are these? They can't be men."

"And they are not women," another said.

"Well, I guess that must be the Middle-sex Regiment!" said a third. (Middlesex County is the home of a famous English military regiment.)

It was, of course the skirt-like dress of the soldiers that led to this funny conversation. The Scottish kilt is the hallmark and the national dress of Scotland, worn by its soldiers and by many Scotsmen around the world, although mainly on national and celebratory occasions.

Scotland is a land of mountains, mists and myths

and many of these last concern the kilt, its origins and the wearing of it. For example, in the popular film *Braveheart*, set in Scotland in the 1200s, the hero William Wallace's freedom fighters wear tartan kilts as though they were the everyday clothes of Scottish Highlanders at that time. But that is not true as it was at least 300 years later, around 1600, that the first evidence of Scotsmen wearing kilted clothes appears, and even these were very different from the modern kilt. Called the *feileadh mor* or great kilt, it was a broad blanket or scarf reaching from the head to the knees and secured at the waist in pleats with a broad belt. It was a century later before the *feileadh beag* or small kilt, which we recognise as the modern-day kilt, was used. This is really the bottom half of the great kilt. This was more convenient for the industrial-type work required as the Highlands were opened to outside exploitation.

By 1745, when Charles Edward Stewart (Bonnie Prince Charlie) fought to regain the British throne for the House of Stewart, the small kilt was largely the standard dress of Highlanders and especially of fighting men. Weavers and dyers of the kilt cloth used many dyes and colours available in their area and many bright and varied colours were woven into the softer shades of mountain and moorland. Thus the clan or area to which the wearer belonged could be seen by the pattern and colours of his kilt. It came about in time that each clan chief and his followers had their own distinctive tartan pattern attached to the name of their clan, such as MacDonald, Cameron, Mackenzie, Murray or Elliott and other similar surnames.

It was really only after the clan system was broken down (by the government as punishment for trying to put Charles Edward Steward on the throne) that the first standardised tartans began to be woven and marketed. Mechanical looms wove the material much faster than hand weavers and kilts could be mass produced. Soon more tartan designs became associated with particular clans, families, regiments and even towns and could be registered as such. Even today, anyone can have a tartan made up to their own design and registered, provided it does not violate another's registered pattern. Kilts were carefully tailored. The pleats were no longer folded by the wearer, but sewn in, making it much quicker and easier to put the kilt on.

The writings of Sir Walter Scott and others, in the early 1800s, added to Scotland's romantic appeal so that tartan became popular in England as well. The kilt became identified with the whole of Scotland rather than just the Highland area. In 1822, King George IV visited Edinburgh. There was a great deal of celebration and there was tartan everywhere. The king himself appeared in a spectacular kilt. His successor, Queen Victoria, loved all things Scottish and dressed her sons in kilts. She also insisted that clan chiefs visiting her wore their clan tartan, even if they did not have one! Many new tartans were without doubt created, or renamed, for the occasion. Clearly, even though the idea of clan tartans was still quite new, the myth already existed that it was very ancient. Now tartan and the kilt is as much if not more than anything else part of Scotland's traditions and almost the 'trademark' of the country.

Visitors to Scotland may be disappointed as they will spot only a few people wearing the kilt as they go about their business. You are, however, almost certain to see the kilt if you go to a Scottish wedding, university graduation or other such celebration. Another place to see the kilt is at the Highland Games. Otherwise, follow the sound of the bagpipes as there is sure to be at least one kilt there!

The kilt, of course, remains part of the uniform of the Scottish Highland military regiments. In World War I, the wild but powerful way of fighting of one Highland regiment led to the German troops who faced them calling them the "Ladies from Hell". While still used as an important feature of the Scottish soldier's uniform on ceremonial and non-combat occasions, the kilt was last worn in action in May 1940 at the battle of Dunkirk in World War II.

Nevertheless, around the world the kilt remains the symbol of Scotland and its people even though it is worn perhaps, even more, by ex-patriot Scots in other lands than in their own Scottish homeland.

苏格兰短裙

韩淑俊 译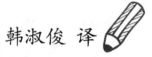

　　据说有这样一个笑话，一队苏格兰士兵行军经过法国的一个村庄时，村民们面面相觑。一个村民说："这是些什么人？他们不可能是男人。"有人接着说："他们也不是女人。"第三个人说："我猜这肯定是中性人军团！"（Middlesex County 字面意为"中性"郡，通常音译为米德尔塞克斯郡，是英国一个著名军团的驻地。）

　　显然，是苏格兰士兵们穿的类似裙子的服装引发了这段令人捧腹的谈话。苏格兰短裙是苏格兰的标志和苏格兰人的民族服饰。苏格兰士兵和世界各地的很多苏格兰人主要在展示民族特色和庆祝场合穿这种服饰。

　　苏格兰是一个重峦叠嶂、雾气缭绕、充满神话色彩的地方。许多神话都涉及苏格兰短裙及其起源和穿着。比如：在以13世纪苏格兰为背景的大片《勇敢的心》中，威廉·华莱士的自由战士们穿的就是格子图案短裙，似乎这种着装就是苏格兰高地居民当时的日常服装。但是情况并非如此，因为苏格兰人穿短裙的最早证据出现在大约1600年，比影片《勇敢的心》所反映的时代至少要晚上300年。而且这种服装与现代的短裙也很不相同。这种衣服叫做"feileadh mor"（盖尔语），即"大格呢褶裙"，这是一种宽宽的毯子或者长围巾，可以从头部一直延伸至膝盖，人们用一条宽腰带将打褶后的衣服固定在腰部。一个世纪之后，人们开始穿"feileadh beag"（盖尔语），即"小格呢褶裙"，也就是我们今天所熟知的苏格兰短裙。它实际上就是大格呢褶裙的下半部分。由于苏格兰高地对外开发，这样的服装样式更便于人们进行工业劳动。

　　到1745年，当查尔斯·爱德华·斯图亚特（邦尼王子查理）为夺回斯图亚特家族的英国王位而战时，小格呢褶裙几乎已经成为苏格兰高地居民，特别是军队士兵的标准服装。纺织工和染工们充分利用当地的各种染料和色彩，将五彩缤纷的鲜亮颜色织入类似山区和沼泽地般柔和色调的布中。这样通过着装者所穿短裙的图案和颜色便可知道他所属的家族或地区。每个部族酋长和他的追随者们逐渐都拥有了专属于自己部族名下的、独一无二的格子图案，这些家族包括麦克唐纳、卡梅伦、麦肯齐、默里和埃利奥特等等。

然而，直到家族制度被废止（政府以此作为对查尔斯·爱德华·斯图亚特复辟的惩罚）之后，最早的标准格子图案才真正开始得以编织和销售。机械织机编织图案要比人工编织快得多，使得短裙的批量生产成为可能。很快，更多的格子图案和特定的部族、家族、军团甚至城镇联系起来，而且还可以进行注册登记。甚至在今天，任何人都可以根据自己的设计制作格子图案并申请注册，但前提是该图案不能和已注册图案发生冲突。当时短裙的缝纫做工极为考究，裙褶都是缝制好的，穿时无需自己打褶，因此穿衣更加快捷容易。

19世纪初期，沃尔特·斯科特爵士及其同时代其他作家的作品为苏格兰平添了许多浪漫的色彩，从而使格子图案在英格兰也大受欢迎。苏格兰短裙被视为整个苏格兰地区而不仅仅是高地地区的象征。1822年，国王乔治四世访问爱丁堡。在欢迎盛典中，苏格兰格子图案随处可见，国王本人也穿了一条别具一格的苏格兰短裙。他的继承人维多利亚女王对苏格兰的一切都情有独钟，她甚至让儿子们穿苏格兰短裙，还坚持要求家族的族长们在拜见她时穿上自己家族特有的格子短裙，即使他们没有也不行！这次拜见，毫无疑问促进了许多新的格子图案的诞生和重新命名。显然，尽管"家族格子"这一概念存在时间不长，但人们误以为它的历史已经很久远了。如今，即使不比其他传统更重要，格子图案和短裙也已成为苏格兰传统的一部分，并且几乎已成为这个国家的标志。

　　游客到苏格兰后可能会感到失望，因为他们很少能见到在日常生活中穿着短裙的苏格兰人。不过，在苏格兰婚礼、大学毕业典礼、其他庆祝活动或者高地运动会上，你肯定会发现穿苏格兰短裙的大有人在；或者你可以顺着风笛声找寻，那么你至少能看到一个穿苏格兰短裙的人！

　　苏格兰短裙仍然是苏格兰高地军团制服的一部分。第一次世界大战时，某个苏格兰高地军团以其骁勇无敌的战术被与其交战的德军称为"地狱来的女士"。1940 年 5 月，在第二次世界大战的敦刻尔克战役中，苏格兰士兵们最后一次在战斗中穿苏格兰短裙。如今苏格兰短裙仍然是苏格兰士兵的特色制服，但只在庆典和非战斗场合穿。

　　然而，苏格兰短裙在全世界依然是苏格兰及其人民的象征，尽管如今穿苏格兰短裙的可能更多的是移居他乡的苏格兰人，而非生活在苏格兰本土的人。

American fashion

Nancy Dickmann

People in the United States wear a huge variety of clothes. From high fashion on the catwalks of New York, to the informal wear seen on the nation's beaches, there are clothes to suit every taste.

Youth fashion

Young people in the United States often dress very informally. Jeans are very popular, and they come in many styles. Blue is the main colour, but you can also get them in white, black and just about any other colour! Jeans can range from very smart, expensive styles, to ones that are old, faded, and patched. It all depends on the look you are trying to achieve!

Many young people wear jerseys that look like those worn by their favourite sports teams. Others wear T-shirts or sweatshirts that have the logo of their school or university, or have the name of a place they have visited. T-shirts with other slogans are also popular, especially with boys.

Baseball caps are popular with both young people and adults. Originally these showed the logo of a baseball team, but now you can get baseball caps that advertise a place, an activity, or even a fashion designer! Trainers are a popular choice of footwear. There are an amazing variety of trainers on offer in shops, and many of them are more fashionable than sporty. The most desirable models can be very expensive.

Business clothes

In a business situation, many men would wear a two-piece suit with a collared shirt and a tie. A woman might wear a smart dress, or a suit, or a skirt and jacket. However, these days many offices have a much less formal dress code. Wearing jeans is often seen as being too casual, but many people might wear a pair of smart trousers and a shirt or jumper. An office with a more formal dress code might have a policy of 'casual Fridays', where one day a week employees can wear less formal clothes. Sometimes the company will ask for a donation to charity in return for this privilege.

Western wear and beach wear

In some parts of the country, Western fashion is widely seen. The most common example is tight jeans worn with a checked shirt, tucked in, and a belt with a big, fancy buckle. The outfit can be topped off with a cowboy hat, sometimes called a 'ten-gallon hat' or 'Stetson', and a pair of pointy-toed leather cowboy boots.

On the beaches, American women wear either a one-piece or a two-piece bathing suit. It is not normally accepted for women to sunbathe topless in the United States. Men will usually wear baggy swimming shorts, often with bright patterns. In the past these shorts were sometimes called 'jams', but now they are commonly called 'board shorts'. They are especially popular with surfers and beach volleyball players.

High fashion

Although most Americans usually dress fairly casually, the country has been home to many famous fashion designers. Some of these names are now famous around the world, such as Calvin Klein, Ralph Lauren, Liz Claiborne, Tommy Hilfiger, and Donna Karan. Younger designers such as Zac Posen are beginning to make their mark, and many of these younger designers focus on more casual clothes than the more traditional designers. The high fashion scene in the United States is centred in New York, where many important fashion magazines are published. New York Fashion Week takes place twice a year, in spring and autumn.

This is an opportunity for many designers to show their new collections.

You will see a wide variety of clothes every time you walk down an American street. There is so much to choose from that everyone can develop their own style!

美国时尚

张华嵩 译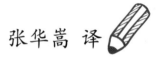

美国人的穿衣风格可谓五花八门。从纽约 T 型台上展示的高级时装，到全国各地海滩上人们的随意穿着，无论你喜欢什么风格，总有一种适合你。

年轻人时尚

美国年轻人的穿着通常很随意。牛仔裤十分盛行，并且呈现多种风格。牛仔裤以蓝色为主，也有白色、黑色和其他几乎任何颜色。牛仔裤可以精美时尚且价格不菲，也可以陈旧褪色还打着补丁。这完全取决于你想要展现什么样的风格。

很多年轻人喜欢穿运动套衫，样式类似他们最喜欢的球队所穿的。有的人穿 T 恤衫或长袖运动衫，上面或印有自己学院或大学的标志，或印着曾游历过的某个地名。印有其他标语的 T 恤衫也很流行，尤其在男孩子中间很受追捧。

棒球帽在年轻人和成人中都很流行。最初，棒球帽仅显示棒球队的标志，而今天你所见到的棒球帽，可能会展示某个地方、宣传某个活动，甚至推介某位时尚设计师！各类鞋子当中，运动鞋非常受青睐。商店出售的运动鞋种类丰富到令人咋舌，其中许多鞋子的时尚性远远超出了其运动性。人气最旺的款式会相当昂贵。

商务着装

在商务场合，很多男士会着两件套西装，内穿带领衬衣，系领带。女士会穿考究的连衣裙或套装，或是半截裙搭配上衣。而如今，很多办公室的着装已经远不那么正规了。穿牛仔裤通常会被认为过于休闲，很多人会穿考究的长裤搭配衬衣或是羊毛衫。着装要求比较正规的办公室通常会实行"周五便装"政策，即一周里有一天，员工可以穿不太正式的服装。有时公司会要求员工进行慈善捐款，作为对这一特权的回报。

西部装束和海滩着装

在美国一些地区，西部时尚随处可见。最常见的例子是紧身牛仔裤搭配格子衬衣，衬衣下摆塞进裤子，外系一条带有硕大花哨搭扣的腰带，再戴上顶牛仔帽（也叫"十加仑帽"或"斯特森毡帽"），穿上尖头牛仔皮靴，这身牛仔行头就完备了。

在海滩，美国女性穿连身或是两件套泳衣。在美国，女性赤裸上身进行日光浴，正常情况下是不被接受的。男士通常会穿着宽松的、带有鲜艳图案的游泳短裤。以前这类短裤有时被称为"睡裤式泳裤"，现在通常被叫做"冲浪裤"，尤其受到冲浪者和沙滩排球爱好者的青睐。

高级时装

尽管大多数美国人通常穿着相当随意，但美国却是很多著名时装设计师的故乡，其中有些已是名扬世界，如卡文·克莱恩、拉尔夫·劳伦、丽诗·加邦、汤米·希尔费格和唐纳·卡伦。年轻一代的设计师如扎克·珀森等已经开始崭露头角。较之更为传统的设计师，很多年轻设计师着力于更加休闲化的设计。美国的高级时装业以纽约为中心，那里也是很多重要时尚杂志的出版地。纽约时装周每年分春、秋两季，是很多设计师展示他们最新设计的大好机会。

每当你漫步在美国街头，总能看到各色各样的着装。各式各样的服饰和搭配随你选择，谁都能穿出自己的风格。

6 Etiquette
礼仪

Don't be late!

James Blanshard

The only thing that British people talk about almost as much as the weather is time-keeping! Most British people like to be on time for things and frown on lateness. They do not like to waste time, and often feel guilty if they delay other people. Most are very apologetic if they are late! Studies often show that the British dislike lateness more than people from any other nation of the world. But why is that?

From a very young age, British people are taught that lateness is wrong. At school, if you are late too often, you may be given a detention. A detention is when you are kept in school during a lunch hour or after school instead of being able to play or go home. In a detention you may be given extra work to do, or you may be asked to do 'lines', which is where you have to write something lots of times, like "I must not be late for class". It is very boring. Have you ever seen the American cartoon *The Simpsons*? At the start, you can see Bart Simpson doing lines on the classroom blackboard!

If you wait at a bus stop or travel by train in the UK, you are sure to see people bustling around, worrying about being late! Public transport in Britain used to have a poor reputation because of lateness, but that is improving. However, buses and trains are still unpredictable, and things like bad weather or accidents often cause delays. To avoid being late in Britain it is best to leave plenty of time to travel, just in case something goes wrong. On the whole though, British people don't mind waiting for things provided they know how long they must wait. But if a timetable is wrong, or a train, aeroplane or bus is very late, there will probably be some complaints!

If you are invited round to a friend's house for a meal, you must do your best to be on time, and if you are going to be late, it is polite to let the host know. It is not always so important to be at parties exactly on time though. At parties, unless you are asked to be on time it is sometimes OK to arrive a little later. However, if you say you can go to the party, but then you can't, it is polite to tell the host.

You should also not phone or visit someone after 10 pm, unless they have asked you to, because most people will think this is too late. If you invite someone to your house at around 6 pm, your guest will probably expect you to offer them some food, and probably a meal. If you invite someone to your house in the afternoon, at, for example, 4 pm, then you should offer them a drink and a cake or a biscuit, not a meal. It helps to avoid confusion.

Since time-keeping is so important to British people, maybe it isn't a surprise that one of the most famous British symbols is a clock. Britain is home to perhaps the most famous clock tower in the world, and maybe the most famous bell. Do you know what it is called? At the Palace of Westminster in London, which is also called the Houses of Parliament, is Big Ben. Big Ben is not actually the clock, but the bell that rings in the clock tower. It has become a popular symbol of Britain, and is often seen in films that are set in London.

The chimes of Big Ben can be heard on British radio and television every day. On New Year's Eve too there is always a big celebration when the bell chimes midnight to ring in the New Year. With Big Ben's famous chimes ringing so loudly in their ears, maybe it is not surprising that British people think time is so important!

切勿迟到！

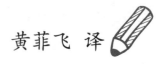

黄菲飞 译

　　在英国人谈论频率较高的话题中，与天气不相上下的只有守时了。大多数英国人喜欢按时做事，对迟到的行为很是反感。他们不愿意浪费时间，如果因为自己的原因耽误了别人的时间，他们会感到内疚。如果迟到了，大多数人会深表歉意。研究结果往往显示，英国人比其他任何国家的人都厌恶迟到。为什么呢？

　　英国人从小就被教导：迟到是不对的。在学校，如果你经常迟到，就可能会被留校。留校意味着你在午饭时间不能出去玩儿，或者放学后不能回家，而必须留在学校里。留校期间，你可能被罚做额外的功课，或是抄句子，也就是说，你必须一遍又一遍抄写同样的东西，比如："我不应该上课迟到。"这种事非常枯燥！你看过美国动画片《辛普森一家》吗？动画一开始，你就会看到巴特·辛普森被罚在教室的黑板上抄句子。

　　在英国，无论是在车站等公交车还是乘火车出行，你总能看到行色匆匆的人们，个个一副担心迟到的样子！以前，英国的公共交通因经常晚点而声名狼藉，但现在情况正在好转！然而，现在公交车和火车的到站时间还是无法预料，诸如恶劣天气和事故之类的事情往往导致晚点。因此，在英国避免迟到的最好方法就是给出行留足时间，省得出岔子！但总的来说，只要能确切地知道需要等待多长时间，英国人并不介意等待。但是如果运行时刻表出现误差，或者火车、飞机或公交车严重晚点，人们可能就要抱怨了！

如果你应邀到朋友家吃饭，那你一定要尽量准时到！如果感觉可能会迟到，要提前通知主人，这样才不会失礼！但是，参加聚会却不必总是准点到达，除非主人明确要求一定要准时，有时迟到一会儿也是可以接受的。但是，如果你答应参加聚会，而随后又不能成行，那你应告知主人，否则就失礼了。

不要在晚上10点以后给别人打电话或者拜访别人，除非你们有约在先，因为多数人都会认为这个时间太晚了！如果你邀请别人在下午6点左右去你家，客人可能以为你会准备一些吃的，并且很可能会留他吃晚饭。如果你邀请别人下午去你家，比如说下午4点，那么你就要请客人喝点东西，吃点蛋糕或饼干，而不用准备晚饭。这些有助于避免误解。

既然守时对英国人如此重要，那么钟成为英国最知名的象征之一就不足为奇了。英国拥有或许是世界上最著名的钟楼和大钟。你知道它的名字吗？它就是坐落在伦敦威斯敏斯特宫即议会大厦的"大本钟"。事实上，大本钟所指的并不是我们通常看到的四面时钟，而是钟楼里敲响的大铜钟。它已经成为了深受人们喜爱的英国标志物，在以伦敦为场景的电影里常常会看到它。

在英国的电台和电视节目中，你每天都能听到大本钟的钟声。新年前夜，大本钟的钟声在午夜时分回响，向人们宣告新年的到来，接着人们就会举行盛大的庆祝活动。有大本钟著名的钟声如此响亮地回荡于耳畔，难怪英国人会这么看重时间！

Fitting in

James and Kate Blanshard

There are lots of unwritten rules about how to behave in a way that people think is right in Britain. It can be difficult for people from other countries to fit in, because lots of British people often do not even realise that they live by these rules until they see someone break them!

If someone invites you to their home for dinner, you should make sure you remember how to behave politely at the dinner table, as mentioned in 'Mealtime manners'. It is also polite to bring a gift for your host if you are invited for a meal, such as chocolates or flowers, to say thank you.

Most people in Britain eat an evening meal at about 6 pm. You should also make sure you do not phone or visit someone at that time in the evening because you will interrupt their meal.

Mealtime invitations are a good way for people to make friends and get to know each other better. When you make friends in Britain, there are some things that you should not say because they are considered rude. It is usually impolite to ask adults how old they are, and traditionally it was particularly offensive to ask a lady her age. Unless you know someone very well, you should not say anything that could be negative about someone's appearance. So, for example, you should not say that they look like they have put weight on. This is offensive in Britain, so you might lose your friend!

British people are well known for being very fussy about queuing. When people are waiting to buy a ticket, or get on a bus, or find a table in a café, they usually form a line to wait until it is their turn. When you arrive, you should join the back of the queue, and make sure you do not push in front of people who have been waiting longer than you. It is rude to push in, and people can get very angry, so you risk being shouted at if you do not wait your turn!

If you are travelling on a bus or train, you must make sure that you queue properly and are polite when you buy your ticket. It is also good manners to offer your seat to someone who is elderly, or has problems walking or standing, or a mother with young children, who is standing. It is also bad manners to drop litter, or chewing gum, instead of putting it in the bin or recycling it. Spitting in the streets, on buses, trains or shops is very impolite in Britain, and is also unhygienic.

Mobile phones and personal music stereos are fun, and handy on long journeys. However, you must be careful about how much noise you make when using them. It is rude to answer your mobile phone if you are already talking to other people, or are eating a meal with others. If you are in a quiet place, like a cinema, museum or church, then your phone should be turned off or turned to silent. People can get upset if you are too noisy. Playing music on your personal stereo or talking too loudly with your friends or on your mobile phone, can make other people annoyed.

Some rules apply to certain places. In school, it used to be good manners for everyone in the class to stand up when an adult entered the room, to show their respect. This is not as common today, but it does still happen in some schools. Children must show their respect to their teacher by calling them by their surname and title, e.g. Mrs Jones, and not by their first name. Children do not call their parents by their first names either. Young children may call their parents 'mummy' and 'daddy' and older children and adults may say 'mum' and 'dad'. They show affection.

Some rules seem a bit silly. Traditionally, British people are good at complaining about things to each other, but not good at telling the people in charge. An example might be where someone in a restaurant ordered a hot meal but it was brought to them cold. They might complain to the people they were eating with, but traditionally would not tell the waiter. They might even tell him everything was fine and that the food was lovely! Today, British people are getting better at complaining when they need to, but some people still think it is a bit rude to complain about something officially.

So, now you know some rules about how to behave you should fit in perfectly—good luck!

入乡随俗

张艳波 译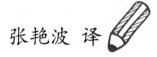

　　在英国，关于得体的行为举止有很多不成文的规矩。这些规矩可能会令外国人很难适应，因为很多英国人也只有在别人违背它们的时候才意识到，其实自己是遵循着这些规矩生活的。

　　如果有人邀请你到他家里共进晚餐，你要切记如何在餐桌上表现得彬彬有礼，就像我们在《餐桌礼仪》一文中介绍的那样。你应邀去别人家用餐时，给主人带上一份礼物，如巧克力或鲜花，以表谢意，这也是礼貌的做法。

大多数英国人的晚餐时间大约是下午 6 点。切忌在这个时间打电话或者拜访某人，因为这可能会打断别人进餐。

邀请别人共同进餐是人们结交朋友和增进彼此间了解的一种很好的方式。在英国，交友时有些事情是不能说的，因为那样别人会认为你很无礼。通常，询问一个成年人的年纪是很不礼貌的，而且依据传统，询问女士的年纪尤其粗鲁。除非你和某人很要好，否则你不应该对其外表作任何负面的评价。比如说：你不能说某人看上去长胖了，这在英国是非常失礼的，你可能会因此失去你的朋友。

众所周知，英国人对排队非常在意。人们在买票、乘公共汽车或在咖啡馆里找位子时，通常都要排队等候。你到了以后，应该主动站到队尾，一定不要插队站到那些比你早到的人前面。插队是令人气愤的无礼行为，所以你如果不排队，可就要当心别人对你大呼小叫了。

乘公共汽车或火车出行的时候，你一定要排队，买票时要有礼貌。给老人、行动或站立不便的人以及带小孩儿的母亲让座是有礼貌的行为。随意丢弃垃圾和口香糖，而不将它们放进垃圾箱或进行回收，是很不文明的举止。在英国，在街道上、公共汽车上、火车上或者商店里吐痰是非常不文明的，也是不卫生的。

长途旅行时，手机和随身听往往能派上用场，给我们带来欢乐。然而，你必须小心，在使用时不要产生太大的噪音。和别人谈话或一起用餐时，接听手机是很不礼貌的。在一些安静的地方，比如电影院、博物馆或教堂，应关闭手机或把手机调成静音。如果你太吵了，别人会不高兴。随身听播放的音乐声音过大，大声地与朋友说话或接听手机，会让别人很恼火。

有些规矩适用于特定的地方。过去在学校里，如果有一位成年人走进教室，学生们礼貌的做法是起立以示敬意。现在这种做法已经不常见了，但在某些学校依然沿用。为了表示尊重，孩子们必须使用姓氏和称谓来称呼他们的老师，比如琼斯太太，而不能直呼其名。孩子们当然也不能直呼父母的名字。年幼的儿童可能叫父母"妈咪"（mummy）和"爹爹"（daddy），年龄较大的孩子和成人可以用"妈妈"（mum）和"爸爸"（dad）的称呼来表达亲昵之情。

有些规矩似乎有些可笑。一般而言，英国人善于向彼此抱怨自己的不满，却不善于将自己的不满讲给责任人听。比如有人在餐馆里点了热餐，但送来的时候却是凉的。他们可能会向一起用餐的人抱怨，但通常不会告诉服务员。他们甚至可能会告诉服务员一切都好，食物非常可口。如今，英国人在必要时已经能够更好地表达自己的不满，但有些人还是认为正式投诉有点儿粗鲁无礼。

那么，现在既然你已经知道了一些行为规则，你就要很好地融入这里的生活。祝你好运！

How do you do?

Nancy Dickmann

When you meet someone new, what should you say? How do you greet a teacher, a parent, or a good friend? There are so many ways to greet people that it is easy to be confused. A greeting might be different, depending on who you are meeting, and the situation.

Greeting words

If you are greeting someone in a formal situation, you might say 'good morning' (or 'good afternoon' or 'good evening'). You would say this to a shopkeeper or a teacher, or an older adult. You could also just say 'hello'. When you meet a person like this for the first time, after you are introduced you should say "Pleased to meet you" or "Nice to meet you". It used to be the custom that after people were introduced, one would ask "How do you do?" But the other person was not supposed to tell them how they were! The correct response would have been to ask "How do you do?" in return. No one actually answers the question in this situation!

Another way to greet someone you don't know very well is to ask "How are you?" Most people will answer this question with something like "Fine, thanks". Even if they are having a bad day, it would be impolite to tell you that! After they tell you how they are, many people will then ask you the same question.

If you are greeting a friend or someone you know well, you can be much less formal. Common words of greeting between friends include 'hi', 'hey', 'hiya' (meaning 'hi, you'), 'hi there', and "What's up?" or "Whassup?" In England you might hear people greet each other by saying 'wotcher' or 'wotcha'. This is an old expression that might originally have started as "What are you up to?" In Australia, many people greet each other with a cheery 'g'day', which is a shortened form of 'good day'. In parts of the United States, you might even hear people say 'howdy', just like a cowboy in a film!

Thank you

If someone does something for you, it is polite to thank them by saying 'thanks' or 'thank you'. A British person might say 'cheers' instead, and this can mean sometimes 'goodbye' as well as 'thank you'. In response, a person might indicate that what they did was no trouble at all by saying 'no problem'.

Gestures for greeting

There are different gestures that go along with the various greeting words. In the past, people might have bowed or curtseyed, and a man would tip his hat to a lady, or kiss her hand. But these are seen as being very outdated now! The most formal gesture used today is a handshake with the right hand. This can be used with business acquaintances, or with a person you don't know very well. It is also common to shake hands with someone when you are introduced to them for the first time.

Adults who know each other well might kiss on the cheek. A man would not usually kiss another man, but a man and a woman, or two women, might kiss cheeks. Although in France it is common to kiss on both cheeks, in Britain it is more usual to just kiss once, on the right cheek. Kissing on the cheek is not very common in the United States. Young people who know each other well will often greet each other with a hug. Others will do a 'high five', where two people slap their upraised right hands.

Writing letters

There are many different ways to start a letter. If it is a business letter to a company where you do not know the name of the person who will read it, it is common to begin with 'To whom it may concern' or 'Dear sir'. If you are writing to a relative or an adult you know well, you would often begin with 'Dear' followed by their first name, or whatever you normally call them, for example 'Dear Uncle John'. If you are writing to a close friend you can be as informal as you like!

问候语

黄菲飞 译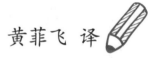

初次与人见面,你该怎么问候?你怎么问候老师、家长或好朋友?问候的方式有很多种,所以人们很容易被弄糊涂。会见的人和场合不同,问候也会有不同的方式。

问候语

如果你是在一个正式场合问候某人,你可以说"早上好"(good morning)、"下午好"(good afternoon)或"晚上好"(good evening)。你可以这样问候一位商店老板、老师或者长者。你也可以只说"你好"(hello)。当你第一次遇到这样的人,在被介绍之后,你应该说

"见到你非常高兴"（Pleased to meet you 或 Nice to meet you）。过去的习俗是在相互介绍之后，一方会问"How do you do?"（字面意思是"你怎么样？"），但是另外一方不会真的告诉他自己怎么样。正确的回答应该是回问"How do you do?"。在这种情况下，没有人会真的回答这个问题的！

另一种问候你不熟识的人的方法是问"你好吗？"（How are you?），大多数人会用类似"很好，谢谢"（Fine, thanks.）这样的话来回答。即使这一天过得非常糟糕，也不能这样告诉别人，否则是很不礼貌的。在别人告诉你他们怎么样之后，很多人会回问你同样的问题。

如果是问候朋友或熟悉的人，你就不必那么拘泥于形式了。朋友之间常见的问候语包括"嗨！"（hi）、"嘿！"（hey）、"你好啊！"（hiya， 即 hi, you)、"嗨，你好啊！"（hi there）和"最近怎么样啊？"（What's up? 或 Whassup?）。在英国，你可能会听到人们互道wotcher 或 wotcha。这是一种古老的表达方式，也许源于"你好吗？"（What are you up to?）。在澳大利亚，许多人会用一句愉快的 g'day! 互致问候，这是"你好！"（good day）的一种简写。在美国的一些地方，你甚至会听到人们说 howdy（"你好"），就像电影中的牛仔一样！

感谢他人

如果有人帮了你的忙，对他说"谢谢"或者"谢谢你"是很礼貌的。英国人可能会说 cheers，这个词语有时意味着"再见"以及"谢谢你"。作为回应，一个人可以说"没什么"（no problem），以表明这么做并没有给自己带来什么麻烦。

问候的动作

不同的问候语会搭配不同的动作。过去，人们打招呼时会鞠躬或行屈膝礼；男士向女士打招呼时则会稍稍举帽，或吻她的手。然而今天，这些都非常过时了！现在最正式的问候方式就是伸出你的右手去和别人握手。无论是和生意场上的熟人，还是不太了解的陌生人，或是初次见面的朋友，你都可以通过握手来表达问候。

熟识的成年人可能会亲吻脸颊以表示问候。一位男士通常不会吻另一位男士，而男士和女士或两个女士之间，则可能会彼此亲吻脸颊。在法国亲吻两颊司空见惯，但在英国，人们通常只吻一下右侧的脸颊。在美国，亲吻脸颊并不常见。相互很熟悉的年轻人常常在问候时给彼此一个拥抱。有些人则会举手击掌，也就是击打彼此举起的右掌。

写信问候

　　写信有很多不同的开头方式。如果你给一家公司写商业信函，但你并不知道谁会来读这封信，此时最常见的开头称呼是"敬启者"（To whom it may concern）或"尊敬的先生"（Dear sir）。如果你给亲戚或相熟的成年人写信，通常应以"亲爱的"开头，紧随其后的是他们的名字，或是任何你通常使用的称呼，例如"亲爱的约翰叔叔"（Dear Uncle John）。如果你给密友写信，那想怎么称呼就怎么称呼啦！

Mealtime manners

James Blanshard

To people in other countries it sometimes seems that British people take table manners very seriously indeed! On television and in films, you often see British people sitting at large dining tables eating formal meals and following strict rules. They usually get most upset when the rules are broken!

In fact, not all mealtimes in the UK are so formal. Those types of meal are rare for most people, except perhaps the Royal family! However, there are some rules that it is helpful to remember whenever you sit down at the table to eat in the UK.

Most British people are taught table manners from a very young age. As soon as they are old enough to hold them, most children are taught how to use a spoon, table knife and fork to cut and eat their food.

When holding your knife and fork, the knife is held in the right hand and the fork is held in the left hand with the points facing down. It is polite to raise the food to your mouth on the back of your fork. Never lick or raise food to your mouth with your knife, and never point your knife or fork at your neighbour, as this is impolite.

But what if you find yourself at a dining table with more than one knife and fork around your plate? Where do you start? This means your meal will begin with a first course, or what is sometimes called a 'starter'. You must use the outer knife and fork for this course.

But before you can begin to eat, it is polite to wait until everyone has been served and has food on their plate. Religious families or groups may also wish to say a prayer of thanks for their food, sometimes called 'Grace', before they begin to eat. It is rude to begin eating before this prayer if the host wishes to say Grace.

When eating, there are a few things to remember. It's polite to wait until you have swallowed your food before speaking to other people or taking more food. Chewing food with your mouth closed is another polite thing to do.

Generally, good manners are to say please and thank you for the meal and to compliment the cook for making the food, telling them how much you enjoyed it. In some countries, a loud belch after a meal is a sign of appreciation to the host, but not in the UK! Burping loudly after a meal is definitely not good table manners in the West.

But remember, table manners are only really important at more formal mealtimes. Often, meals are not so formal and it's OK to eat food with your fingers, not a knife and fork. For example, if you buy chips from a fish and chip shop, and there is no table to sit at, table manners don't apply! However, eating the fish with your fingers could get messy, so most chip shops also have small wooden or plastic forks to take away.

Burgers and pizza are often eaten with the fingers too, though pizza is never eaten with the fingers in Italian restaurants, where it is eaten with a knife and fork.

Sometimes, formal occasions like weddings and parties have 'finger food'. Finger food is usually small pastries, or savoury bread snacks, sandwiches, and sometimes pieces of chicken. It is fine to eat these with your fingers.

However, even if you are eating food with your fingers, you must still be careful not to drop it. And you are certainly never allowed to throw food. That would definitely not be good manners!

餐桌礼仪

黄菲飞 译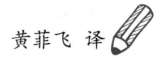

在其他国家的人们看来，英国人有时似乎过于注重餐桌礼仪。在电视节目或者电影中，你经常能看到英国人在一张大餐桌前正襟危坐地吃正餐，每个人都严格遵守餐桌礼仪；如果有人违反了相关礼仪，他们通常会十分不快。

实际上，在英国并非所有的吃饭时间都是如此正式。也许除了王室成员，大多数人很少有机会经历这种严格遵循餐桌礼仪的正餐场合。然而，你在英国就餐时，记住一些餐桌礼仪还是十分有用的。

大多数英国人在很小的时候就接受餐桌礼仪的教导。当孩子们会拿餐具时，大人们就开始教他们如何使用勺子，如何用刀叉切割食物和进餐。

你手持刀叉时，要右手拿刀，左手拿叉，而且刀叉尖要朝下。用叉子背面将食物送到口中是礼貌的举止。千万不能舔食物或用餐刀将食物送入口中，也不要用刀叉指着你的邻座，那是非常不礼貌的。

假如你发现餐桌上有不止一副刀叉放在餐盘旁边

的时候，你该怎么做呢？应该先使用哪副刀叉呢？这意味着你的这顿饭要从第一道菜开始吃，第一道菜有时被称为"开胃菜"。这时候，你必须使用摆在最外侧的刀叉吃第一道菜。

在就餐之前，你一定要等到餐桌上每个人的饭菜都上齐了，然后再开始用餐，这才是礼貌的。宗教家庭或者团体在吃饭前还会做祷告，感谢上帝赐给他们食物，这种饭前祷告有时也被称为"谢恩祈祷"。如果主人想做谢恩祷告，你在此之前就开始用餐是十分无礼的。

在吃饭时还有几点需要注意。等到将口中的食物咽下后，再和别人说话或者再取食物，这是礼貌的行为。吃东西的时候要闭嘴咀嚼，这也是礼貌的举止。

一般而言，礼貌的言行还包括使用"请"、"谢谢"之类的字眼，称赞为你准备食物的厨师，告诉对方你多么喜欢吃他们做的饭菜。在有些国家，饭后打一个响亮的饱嗝是对主人的恭维，但在英国可千万别这么做。在西方国家，饭后打响嗝绝对是很不礼貌的行为。

然而也要记住，餐桌礼仪只有在比较正式的就餐场合中才显得尤其重要。通常情况下，就餐没有那么正式，不用刀叉而用手拿着食物吃也是可以的。比如说：如果你从一家卖炸鱼薯条的小店里买了炸薯条，而店里没有桌子可以让你坐在那儿吃，这时就谈不上餐桌礼仪了。不过，用手拿着炸鱼吃会把手弄脏，所以很多薯条店会附送可以带走的小号木叉或塑料叉子。

人们也常用手直接拿着汉堡和比萨饼吃。然而在意大利餐厅，人们从来不用手拿着比萨饼吃，而是使用刀叉。

有时候，在一些正式的场合，如婚礼或聚会，也会供应手抓小食品，一般有小糕点、开胃面包小吃、三明治，有时还会有鸡块。此时，你完全可以用手拿着这些东西吃。

不过，即使是用手拿着食物吃，你也要小心别让食物掉下来。而且你绝不能乱丢食物，那绝对是不礼貌的。

7 Education
教育

British school life

James Blanshard

They say in the UK that 'your schooldays are the best days of your life', so school is very popular! There are many different types of school in Britain. You don't have to pay to go to school in the UK, but some—called 'public' or 'private' schools—do charge fees. Private schools are often 'boarding schools', which means the children sleep there. A famous boarding school is Eton, where the royal princes William and Harry studied. Most schools though are free to attend, as long as you live nearby. It is the law in the UK that everybody has to study until they are 16.

Most children begin to go to nursery school in the UK when they are aged three or four. At nursery school children will begin to learn how to count and read.

They may learn the English alphabet, and do lots of crafts and games.

The next step, at the age of about five years old, is primary school. You can read about what a first day at primary school is like in another part of this book. Starting primary school can be scary, but most children find they make friends quickly and soon begin to enjoy themselves. Bullying is not allowed, and most teachers are not too strict!

Primary school is more formal than nursery. At primary school children begin to learn how to listen carefully and behave well. They are often given books to read and are encouraged to take them home to read with their parents too.

As well as learning to read and write, children at primary school in the UK may begin to learn about other places in the world—perhaps even China! They may try speaking another language, like French or Spanish, too.

Primary school children will also do drama and singing, and will be able to try lots of types of art—perhaps painting, making models and sewing. Some primary schools encourage children to learn how to play a musical instrument. This might begin with a small recorder, which sounds a little bit like a whistle. Older children may try brass and stringed instruments, like the violin.

Primary schools in the UK are often well-equipped with computers. All the children should get the chance to learn how computers work, and how to use a mouse and keyboard. They may also get to try using the Internet, and may even put some of their work on a website!

Primary schools will also teach their children about animals, different materials and other scientific things. They may learn how plants grow, and how machines work.

At primary school there are plenty of chances to play games and sports. Most schools have football, netball and other sports teams, and everyone is encouraged to take part.

At the age of 11, most children then go to a secondary school. At secondary school, children often move from one classroom to another during the day, rather than be taught all the subjects in the same place. It can be tricky finding your way around the school at first, especially if it is a big school with lots of students!

At secondary school, children will begin to learn about different types of science, like physics, chemistry and biology. They may begin to have lessons to learn a different language (most often French or German) and could start to learn about history, geography and religious education too. All secondary schools see English and maths lessons as being extra important, because they help all of the other subjects.

At the end of secondary school, students take important exams. These give the students qualifications, which help them to get jobs, or go on to do more study at college or university. After the age of 16, it is no longer the law that you have to study, but many people do.

British schools can be a lot of fun! There are lots of things to learn and new friends to make.

英国校园生活

张艳波 译

　　在英国，人们常说"学生时代是一生中最美好的时光"，因此，上学颇受青睐。英国的学校种类繁多，一般都是免费就读的，但一些"公学"或"私立学校"则是收费的。私立学校通常实行"寄宿制"，要求学生在学校住宿。伊顿公学是英国一所著名的寄宿学校，英国皇室的威廉王子和哈里王子曾经在这里就读。大多数学校对于住在学校附近的居民都实行免费教育。英国法律规定，16岁以下的孩子必须上学接受教育。

在英国，大多数儿童3~4岁开始上幼儿园。他们在幼儿园开始学习数数和阅读，还会学习英文字母，做很多手工和游戏。

接下来，大概到5岁时，就该上小学了。在本书的另一篇文章中，您将了解到在英国小学第一天上学的情况。孩子刚开始上学时可能会感到害怕，但是大多数孩子都会很快交到朋友，并开始喜欢上校园生活。学校严禁恃强凌弱，大多数老师也不是特别严厉。

小学比幼儿园更正规一些。在小学阶段，学生开始学习如何认真听讲并规范自己的言行举止。学校经常会给学生一些阅读书目，并鼓励他们把书带回家和父母一起阅读。

除了学习读写之外，英国的小学生还可能开始了解世界其他国家，甚至可能是中国的情况。他们可能去尝试学习外语，如法语或西班牙语。

小学生还要学习戏剧表演、唱歌，并能够尝试许多种其他方面的技艺，如绘画、模型制作和缝纫。一些小学鼓励学生学习弹奏乐器，他们可能会从一种声音类似哨音的小竖笛学起，大点儿的孩子则会尝试铜管乐琴和小提琴等弦乐器。

英国的小学通常配备了完善的电脑设施，每个孩子都有机会亲身体验电脑是如何运行的，以及如何正确使用鼠标和键盘。他们还会学习如何上网，甚至会把他们的一些作品放到网站上。

小学阶段，学生还要学习识别各种动物、不同的材料以及其他科普知识。他们可能还会学习植物的生长过程以及机器的运行原理。

小学阶段，学生有很多机会玩各种游戏和参加各种体育活动。大多数学校都有足球队、无挡板篮球队和其他运动队，学校鼓励每个学生参与其中。

大多数孩子在 11 岁时进入中学学习。在中学，学生们通常需要在一天内不断换教室上课，而不是一直坐在同一个教室里学习所有的课程。因此，一开始学生可能需要费很大劲才能找到要去的地方，尤其是在那些学生人数很多的大学校。

中学阶段，学生开始学习各种科学课程，如物理、化学和生物。他们也可能开始学习一门外语（通常是法语或德语）或历史、地理及宗教教育等课程。中学都非常重视英语课和数学课，因为这两门课有助于其他课程的学习。

中学毕业时，学生要参加一些重要的考试，以取得相应的资格证书。这些证书有助于他们找工作或申请大学。法律不再要求 16 岁以上的孩子继续接受教育，但是很多人还是会选择继续上学。

　　英国的学校生活很有趣。在这里，学生不仅能学到很多东西，还会结交到很多新朋友。

School in the United States

Nancy Dickmann

In the United States, having an education is very important. All children attend school and most people view education as the best way to achieve success in life. The government provides free education up to the age of 18. Most students attend public schools, but about 10 per cent of parents choose to pay to send their children to private schools.

Age levels

Some children begin what is called 'pre-school' as early as age three, but most children start school at the age of five. This is called 'kindergarten', a German word that means 'garden of children'! After kindergarten, each year group is assigned a grade number, from first grade all the way up through twelfth grade. In the past, a school might have included all 12 grades, but this is very rare now. A school like that would probably be found in a rural area with a small number of students. In most places schools are divided into elementary, middle, and high schools. Elementary schools normally include kindergarten plus first through fifth grade. Sixth, seventh and eighth grades are part of 'middle school', and grades nine through twelve will be completed at a high school.

After high school, students can choose to continue their education, but it is no longer free. They can go to a college or university. Some programmes are two years long, but most are four years, and the student attains a bachelor's degree at the end. After that, some students go on to earn a master's degree or even a doctorate.

Classes and exams

In elementary school, most classes will have between twenty and thirty students. If it is a big school, there might be several classes at the same grade level. Most children hope to be placed in the same class as their friends, or with a teacher that they like. But it doesn't always work out that way! At elementary school, students study reading, spelling, maths, science, social studies (a mixture of geography and history), music, art and physical education. Tests in reading and maths make sure that the teachers are doing a good job.

In middle school, children study the same subjects as in elementary school, but they might be able to choose other subjects, such as learning a musical instrument or a foreign language. In high school all students study science, maths, English, and social science, and most students learn a language such as French, Spanish or German. They must take exams in their final year if they want to apply for college or university.

A typical school day

Some public schools have required uniforms, but many don't. Even so, students have to look neat and tidy. Many schools run big yellow buses to bring children to school. Other students walk or ride their bicycles to get to school. A few students come by car with their parents.

During elementary school, children attend classes for about six hours a day. They will stay in the same classroom for most of that time, with a teacher who teaches most of the subjects. For classes such as physical education or music, they go to a special classroom, and they might share these lessons with students from other classrooms. Lunch is provided in the school cafeteria. There will be hot meals available to buy, but many students choose to bring a 'sack lunch' from home. After lunch there is normally a break period called 'recess', when children can play outside. Some children would say that recess is their favourite part of the day!

School usually finishes around 3 pm. Students will often take part in activities after school, such as a sports team. Other students might be part of a club. In the evening, students often have to do homework. A first grader might only have 15 minutes or so of homework to do, while a fifth grader could have more than an hour. High school students have even more!

美国的学校

张艳波 译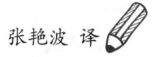

在美国，接受教育非常重要。每个孩子都要上学，因为多数人都认为教育是人生获得成功的最好途径。政府为 18 岁以下的孩子提供免费教育。多数学生上公立学校，但有大约 10% 的父母花钱送孩子上私立学校。

年龄级别

有些孩子早在 3 岁就开始上幼儿园，但多数孩子 5 岁才开始上学。这个阶段被称为幼儿园，即 "kingdergarten"，这是个德语词，意思是 "孩子的乐园"。幼儿园教育之后，学生按照入学年份分组，每组会被分配一个年级数，从一年级一直到十二年级。过去，一所学校可能包括所有十二个年级，但现在这样的学校已为数不多了，只有在学生数量很少的农村地区才可能存在。在多数地方，学校分为小学、初中和高中。小学通常包括幼儿园和一至五年级，初中从六年级到八年级，而高中是从九年级一直到十二年级。

高中毕业后，学生可以选择是否继续求学，但之后接受的教育不再免费。他们可以上专业学院或综合大学，有些专业只有两年，但大部分都是四年，学生完成学业后可以获得学士学位。之后，一些学生继续攻读硕士甚至博士学位。

班级和考试

在小学，大部分班级通常有二三十个学生。规模比较大的学校里，同一年级会有几个班。多数孩子都希望和自己的朋友分到同一个班或遇到他们喜欢的老师，但并不是总能如愿！小学课程包括阅读、拼写、数学、自然科学、社会科学（融合了地理和历史方面的知识）、音乐、艺术和体育。阅读和数学课的测试可以确保任课老师的教学质量。

初中课程和小学课程相同，但初中生还可以选择其他科目，譬如学一种乐器或一门外语。所有的高中生都要学习自然科学、数学、英语和社会科学，多数学生还要学习一门外语，如法语、西班牙语或德语。

如果他们想申请专科学院或综合大学，就必须在高中最后一年参加相应的考试。

一个典型的上学日

一些公立学校有统一的校服，但许多学校都没有。即使没有校服，学生们也必须穿戴整洁。许多学校都有黄色大巴接学生到校，其他学生则步行或骑自行车上学，也有少数学生搭乘父母的汽车上学。

小学生每天大约上课六小时，他们大部分时间都在同一间教室里，由一位老师教授大部分课程。而对于体育或音乐这样的课程，他们则需要到一间专门的教室，还可能和其他班的学生一起上课。学校的自助餐厅提供午餐，有许多热气腾腾的饭菜可供购买。但许多学生都选择从家带袋装午餐。午饭之后通常有段休息时间，叫做"课间休息"，孩子们可以在教室外玩耍。一些孩子会说，课间休息是他们一天中最喜欢的时间段！

学校通常下午三点左右放学，之后学生经常会参加一些活动，如运动队，有些学生可能参加某个俱乐部。晚上学生通常需要写作业，一年级学生的作业量大约需要 15 分钟时间完成，五年级学生可能要一个多小时，而高中生则需要更多时间。

My first day at Lenton Primary

Gu Lantian

On August 28, 2003, I went to Nottingham, a city in central England, with my parents. We lived in Lenton District and Mum and Dad decided to send me to an old school called Lenton Primary.

September 3 was my first school day in England. I felt really nervous when I entered the school gate. The school area was very small, and there were only three old buildings made of dark red bricks and a simple playground, but they looked warm and friendly.

I stood timidly at the end of the line of the third-years. A few minutes later, a plump lady with black hair and dark skin led us into a classroom (Later I got to know that the lady was our class teacher, Ms Latif). The floor of the classroom was covered with blue carpet. At one end there was a chair for the teacher and behind it a white board. In the middle there were a few desks and chairs for the students. The students did not sit rigidly in rows, but quite casually around the desks and they could move freely even when the teacher was talking. On the walls there were many photos of the students and some maps as well. When I finally took in all the things in the classroom, our first lesson started. Ms Latif said a long sentence in English. All my classmates started writing at once. Only I was at a loss as to what to do, for I didn't understand a word of what Ms Latif had just said! I peeped at the boy sitting beside me. He was writing in his notebook "My name is James..." Oh, so I was supposed to write a self-introduction.

After everyone finished their introduction, Ms Latif called us together and we lined up and went out of the classroom. We crossed the playground and entered a large hall. All the other classes were already sitting on the floor, cross-legged. I had a count and found out that there were about 100 students altogether! Soon a middle-aged man walked to the front and began to speak—he was, Mr Magner, our headmaster. He talked for quite some time and asked many questions, for which the students held up their index finger to answer.

Finally the assembly ended and we went back to our classroom to resume our class. First we had maths—it was so much easier than what I learned in China, and the atmosphere in class was so much more relaxed and friendly than that in Beijing. What is more, at Lenton Primary, their way of teaching maths was also very different from that in Beijing. For example, they didn't force the students to memorise the multiplication table. Instead they asked the students to work out the table themselves.

After the maths class, all my classmates stormed out of the classroom into the playground. In Beijing we just had ten minutes between classes, but the between-classes break at Lenton Primary was half an hour! We played cricket, football, rugby, tennis and all kinds of sports. It was really more or less a sports lesson!

We had one more class in the morning and then it was lunchtime. Our dining hall was the same hall in which we had our assembly. A huge buffet was laid out and the food was great. There were chips, sandwiches, baked beans, fried chicken, salad, ice cream, jelly… I followed my classmates and queued with a tray in my hand, and when it was my turn, I piled the tray with a bit of everything.

After lunch there was a long playing session. I played football with some other boys—something quite unthinkable in Beijing, where the students were prevented from going to the playground at noon. They were expected to do their homework in the classroom. We had two classes in the afternoon and at 3:20 Mum came and picked me up.

This was my first school day in England. I had nice surprises, I also had worries. Soon I made a lot of friends in my class. At the end of the first month, I was able to follow all the courses and by the end of the first term, I was already one of the top students in English, maths and science.

我在英国上学的第一天

顾蓝天 文

2003 年 8 月 28 日，我和爸爸妈妈来到了英格兰中部的诺丁汉市。我们一家住在兰顿区。爸爸妈妈为我联系了一所历史悠久的小学 —— 兰顿小学。

9 月 3 日，我怀着既兴奋又紧张的心情踏进了这所学校的大门。校园很小，只有二三栋平房和一个简陋的操场，却给人一种温馨的感觉。

我胆怯地站在三年级的队尾，没过一会儿，出来一位胖胖的中年妇女，黑头发，棕色皮肤，后来我才知道她是拉提夫女士，是我们的班主任。我跟着队伍走进教室，发现这里的教室铺着蓝地毯，教室的一端放着一把教师专用的椅子，椅子后面是白板。教室中间有几张课桌和几把椅子，供学生们使用。学生们没有严格地按排就座，而是围着课桌随意地坐着。他们甚至在老师讲课时还可以自由活动。墙上挂了许多学生的照片，还有一些地图。我将教室打量完后，就开始上课了。拉提夫女士说了一句很长的话，我拼命地猜，也没猜出她说的是什么意思。同学们马上开始写起来。我瞅了一眼同桌的本子，只见上面写着"我的名字叫詹姆斯——"这才恍然大悟，原来老师是让我们写自我介绍，于是我也硬着头皮在本子上写起来。

过了一会儿，同学们都站起来跑到教室门口排队，我看大家都那么兴高采烈的样子，心想一定是下课了，也就跟着他们跑到队伍里。拉提夫女士领着我们出了教室，走过操场，进到一个大大的礼堂里，别的年级的同学已经在那里坐好了。原来还没到下课时间，全校学生都到礼堂里参加每天上午的集会。我学着大家的样子盘腿席地而坐，抬眼一看，讲台上还站着一位穿着笔挺的西服、脑门儿光秃秃的男士。后来我才知道他是我们的校长麦格纳先生。不一会儿，麦格纳先生开始讲话，而我就像听天书一样，一句也不懂。麦格纳先生还问了好多问题，我身边的同学们一个一个举起食指踊跃发言。

好不容易盼到全校集会结束了，我跟着我们班的队伍回到自己的教室，开始上数学课。虽然我还是什么也听不懂，但是老师写在黑板上的阿拉伯数字和各种加减算式我可是清清楚楚。比起我们在中国学的内容，英国小朋友学的数学实在太简单了，但是他们有一些特别的推算方式很有意思，比如：乘法口诀表英国老师就不要求同学们背诵，而是自己推算出来。

数学课之后是我们的第一个大课间。我随着同学们跑到操场上。呵！操场上可真热闹！有的在玩板球，有的在踢足球，还有打网球的、跳绳的，个个都玩得热火朝天。我是一个足球迷，自然就加入了踢足球的那一伙儿。这个大课间可真长啊，足足有半个小时，我们都玩得特别尽兴。

一上午的时间就这样伴随着听天书一般的课程和热闹的课间很快过去了。该吃午饭了，我和同学们跑进大厅里，我惊讶地发现我们开会的大厅不知什么时候已经变成饭厅了，摆着整整齐齐的桌椅，飘着诱人的食物的香味。英国学校的午餐和我们中国的盒饭不一样，吃的是自助餐。我学着同学们的样子拿了一个托盘，走到摆满食物的长桌旁。哇，那么多好吃的，真是让我眼花缭乱！有土豆条、金枪鱼三明治、番茄酱烤黄豆、炸鸡腿，还有水果沙拉、冰激凌、果冻……真是数都数不过来。我每样取了一些，然后找了个座位坐下，开始舞动刀叉大吃大喝起来。

午饭之后是长长的午休——不是要大家睡觉，而是到操场上照玩不误。下午上的是科学课，我自然还是一个"长着耳朵的聋子"。但是我使出浑身解数认真听讲，你别说，偶尔还能捕捉住一两个单词。下午3:20，放学的时间到了。一走出教室，我就看见妈妈微笑着站在院子里等我，便跑过去一头扑进妈妈的怀里。

这就是我在英国上学的第一天，有惊喜，也有苦恼。后来我跟很多同学成了好朋友。一个月以后，我已经能听懂所有的课程；第一个学期结束时，我在英语、数学和科学方面都是班里的尖子了。

Summer camps

Lan Chun

Lancaster University organised a series of summer camps with different themes for children of different age groups. William enrolled for two of them. One was a sports camp, and the other a science and arts camp called 'Time Out'. From the day he registered, William had been looking forward eagerly to the opening of his camps. Kidding him, I said I had never seen him so looking forward to his school life in Beijing, and he answered, "Well, they have such nice teachers here. They never shout at students. I just know the summer camps here will be great fun and not like the camps in Beijing where you are always expected to learn something." Not knowing what to say, I just smiled.

The sports camp opened on July 28. We started off at 9 o'clock. William was well-equipped with his swimming suit in his backpack and his packed lunch (a sandwich, a cup of yogurt, a cereal bar and an apple) in his hand. He was absolutely radiating with excitement. When I picked him up at 5 o'clock in the evening, seeing me, he simply burst out "Oh, Mum, I'm totally exhausted!", and at once I knew he had had a fantastic day!

He retold all the details to me over dinner. "We tried boxing in the morning." "What? Boxing?" "Oh yes. We've got a coach and I have learned a lot from him." He put down his knife and fork and demonstrated a left jab for me. "Mum, I think this is very useful. I shall try it when we go back to Beijing." "Please, on whom do you plan to try it?" "Oh, Mum, don't you know that self-defence is very important?"

He had a few more chips and resumed his babbling. "Some of the boys went crazy over my trainers. They asked me if they could touch them, and one of the boys even commented that the trainers must be made of gold. I told him that they are definitely made of rubber." I said, "You must have really disappointed them." That pair of brand new Nike trainers William was wearing was a gift from his grandparents. Later I emailed William's grandparents and told them about the sensation caused by the trainers. They were greatly amused.

At the end of the second day, William told me, "We played table tennis in the morning. The bats were so poor that they really didn't help me doing well, but I still beat them all. The coach, then, played with me and won a game, but it was close." He paused for a while and added shyly, "The two coaches got very interested in me and asked me which school I attended. They wanted to enroll me on their team, but I told them I'm from China and they were quite disappointed."

Football, tennis, badminton, cricket, rugby, hockey, swimming… and a trip to the Magic Kingdom of Camelot made this sports camp a paradise for sporty children like William. On seeing him coming home every day radiating with happiness, I couldn't help asking myself: When can Chinese schools and Chinese teachers give Chinese children such a free and happy and colourful holiday?

The second camp William joined, called 'Time Out', was more oriented to science and arts. To my surprise, he looked angry and depressed on coming home at the end of the first day. Below is his diary:

August 4, Monday

Today is my first day at the Time Out camp. In the morning we introduced ourselves to each other and played a few games like 'Murder Wink', 'Yes and No', etc. I had a jolly good time.

After lunch, I played with a half British half Japanese boy called Joe. He lent me his DS and we played football games on it. Then the afternoon session started. A teacher called Kate came to teach us art. She told us art meant different things to different people and asked us to make a poster about the most British things in small groups. She gave each group a piece of paper to draw with and some newspapers which could give us some ideas about British things.

I opened a newspaper and found a page about the coming Olympic Games in Beijing. At the top of the page there was a big photo showing a Chinese policeman trying to block a camera. A boy beside me pointed at the photo and said, "They are bad people who kill others, aren't they?" I said no and told him that is a lie of the Western media. Then he said something about Dalai Lama. I told him that Dalai is a liar too. He thought I was being very stupid and told the other boys that I said Dalai was bad. They all looked shocked. So I told them that they were receiving false information from the BBC and other Western media. I told them the story of Jin Jing, a disabled athlete. During the Olympic torch relay in Paris, some people under Dalai's control attacked her and tried to snatch her torch. Then the teacher Kate joined in and said that I was receiving false information from the Chinese media.

At this point I got really cross, but I managed to keep my cool. I said I didn't blame them for holding false information about China because we Chinese people haven't done enough to help them know about our country.

I said, "If you have been to China, you will find that it is not as polluted as you thought, and it is much more developed than the BBC has had you believe."

That night William tossed and turned in his bed for a long time. He said to me like an adult, "Mum, now I understand what you told me before: If we want the world to understand China, people like us who have opportunities to go abroad need to try our best." I asked him if he would like me to have a word with his camp teachers. He said, "No, I think I can cope with it."

The days that followed turned out to be smooth and uneventful. On Tuesday, the children made rockets out of paper under the supervision of a professor from the Physics Department. They then launched their rockets in the courtyard. They also painted their own chinaware under the supervision of a professor from the Arts Department. On Wednesday, the children made their own ice cream using liquid nitrogen (William reassured me that the ice cream tasted "really good") and studied the history of World War I together. On Thursday a local band came with a truck loaded with all sorts of strange musical instruments. Each child was assigned two notes and an instrument and was asked to compose a tune. On Friday, the children went to the sports centre on campus and tried all sorts of aquatic games…

On the last day of the camp, the chinaware painted by the children was baked, packed and delivered to each child. What William made was a dark blue plate with a very abstract geometric figure in the middle. I asked him what that figure meant. He just smiled, but did not answer.

夏令营

蓝纯 文

　　兰卡斯特大学为孩子们组织了一些夏令营活动，我给儿子报了其中的两个。一个是 sports camp，另一个是名为 Time Out 的 science and arts camp，各为期一周。从报名之日起，儿子就掰着手指头期待着。我挪揄地说，在北京从来没见你这么盼着上学啊，儿子答："这儿的老师好啊，不像北京的老师那么凶，而且我知道这儿的夏令营就是为了让我们玩儿好！不像北京的夏令营总是学这个学那个。"呵呵，一时无语。

　　7 月 28 号是 sports camp 开营的日子。9 点，我送儿子出门。儿子背着双肩包（内装浴巾、泳裤、泳镜），拎着盒饭（一份三明治、一份配巧克力豆的酸奶、一块脆米棒、一个苹果），雄赳赳，气昂昂。下午接儿子，他见到我的第一句话是："Oh, Mum, I'm totally exhausted!（哦，妈妈，我是真累啊！）"语气里透出的却是掩饰不住的兴奋。

吃晚饭时，他跟我絮叨一天的种种细节："上午我们练拳击来着。"我吃了一惊："拳击？""对啊。有一个教练专门教我们，我学了好几招呢。"说着就放下饭碗比划给我看，又憧憬道："我觉得这几招特有用，等回北京了就能用上。""啊？你要用在谁身上啊？""妈妈，你不知道自卫能力是很重要的吗？"

停了停，儿子又说："Some of the boys went crazy over my trainers. They asked me if they could touch them, and one of them even commented that the trainers must be made of gold. I told him that they are definitely made of rubber."我笑了："你就不能骗骗他吗？"儿子那双鞋是新款的耐克，是姥姥姥爷送给他的小学毕业礼物，引起这样的轰动效应却是出乎我们的意料。

第二天，儿子回来告诉我："今天上午打乒乓球了。他们的拍子巨烂（注：儿子在家里有一副极好的拍子），影响我发挥，不过我还是把他们都打败了。后来教练上来跟我对打，扳回一局。"停了停，又不好意思地补充说："The two coaches got very interested in me and asked me which school I attended. They wanted to enroll me on their team, but I told them I'm from China and they were quite disappointed."

足球、网球、羽毛球、板球、橄榄球、曲棍球……还有每天都少不了的游泳，以及去"卡米洛魔幻王国"（类似北京的欢乐谷）旅行了一次，这个 sports camp 可谓名副其实。什么时候我们的学校和老师也能让我们的孩子这样投入地玩儿一回呢？

风波

　　如果说 sports camp 以动为主，那么 Time Out 则以静为本（自夸一句：俺在选择夏令营时就想到要动静结合的）。没想到第一天儿子回家竟有些义愤填膺，下面是他当天奋笔疾书的日记：

August 4, Monday

Today is my first day at the Time Out camp. In the morning we introduced ourselves to each other and played a few games like 'Murder Wink', 'Yes and No', etc. I had a jolly good time.

After lunch, I played with a half British half Japanese boy called Joe. He lent me his DS and we played football games on it. Then the afternoon session started. A teacher called Kate came to teach us art. She told us art meant different things to different people and asked us to make a poster about the most British things in small groups. She gave each group a piece of paper to draw with and some newspapers which could give us some ideas about British things.

I opened a newspaper and found a page about the coming Olympic Games in Beijing. At the top of the page there was a big photo showing a Chinese policeman trying to block a camera. A boy beside me pointed at the photo and said, "They are bad people who kill others, aren't they?" I said no and told him that is a lie of the Western media. Then he said something about Dalai Lama. I told him that Dalai is a liar too. He thought I was being very stupid and told the other boys that I said Dalai was bad. They all looked shocked. So I told them that they were receiving false information from the BBC and other Western media. I told them the story of Jin Jing, a disabled athlete. During the Olympic torch relay in Paris, some people under Dalai's control attacked her and tried to snatch her torch. Then the teacher Kate joined in and said that I was receiving false information from the Chinese media.

At this point I got really cross, but I managed to keep my cool. I said I didn't blame them for holding false information about China because we Chinese people haven't done enough to help them know about our country. I said, "If you have been to China, you will find that it is not as polluted as you thought, and it is much more developed than the BBC has had you believe."

那天晚上，儿子一直辗转反侧，难以入睡。他跟我说："妈妈，现在我明白你以前跟我说的话了：要想让世界了解中国，像我们这样有机会走出国门的中国人就应该尽自己的努力。"我问他要不要我去跟夏令营的老师沟通一下，他说不用，"I think I can cope with it."

接下来的几天风平浪静。星期二，孩子们在物理系教授的指导下用纸做火箭，还拿到院子里去发射；在艺术老师的指导下手绘陶瓷器皿；星期三，孩子们品尝了用液化氮制作的冰激凌；一起讨论第一次世界大战的历史；星期四，来自附近城市一个乐队的乐手带来一卡车稀奇古怪的乐器，按照每个孩子名字的首写字母给他们指定两个音符，让他们编一首乐曲；星期五，去 sports centre 玩水上游戏……

夏令营结束时，每个孩子手绘的陶瓷器皿都烧制好了，经过细心包装之后发给了孩子。儿子做的是一个深蓝色的盘子，中间画着一个相当抽象的几何图案。问他那图案是什么意思，他却笑而不答。

8 Sports
体育

Popular sports in the UK

James Blanshard

The UK is a famous place for sports, and some of the world's best sportsmen and women are from there. Almost all of the world's sports are played in the UK, so whatever sport you like, there is certain to be someone in the UK to play with!

The UK is home to the oldest soccer team in the world (Notts County FC), the oldest tennis tournament (Wimbledon), and it's the place where cricket and rugby were invented, and is where many sports first had their rules written down.

Team sports played by groups are more popular than individual sports. Football (or soccer) is definitely the most popular team game. In towns and cities, you will find football players on almost every spare patch of grass trying to kick the ball into the goal past a diving goalkeeper!

To show how important football is in the UK, Bill Shankly, a manager of Liverpool FC in the 1960s, said, "Football is not a matter of life and death. It's far more important than that." Lots of football fans in the UK feel the same way!

Manchester United, Liverpool, Arsenal and Chelsea are some of the best teams in England. To play for those teams you have to be one of the greatest players in the world! Rangers and Celtic in the Scottish Premier League have some excellent players too.

Rugby is another team sport, like football, that is played all over the UK and the world. Rugby is the national sport of Wales, so they have one of the best teams. In rugby, players throw and carry an egg-shaped ball, dodging opponents that try to catch them and tackle them to the ground. Often, rugby players end up in a big muddy heap of bodies with the ball somewhere beneath!

Legend has it that rugby was invented at a school in England by a mischievous schoolboy called William Webb Ellis. He was playing football but he didn't enjoy it, so instead he picked up the ball and ran with it!

In the summer time, when the rugby and football seasons have ended, lots of English people enjoy watching a game of cricket. Cricket is a ball game played between two teams. It's very popular, but also very confusing if you don't know the rules.

Cricket has a language all of its own. Funny sounding words and phrases like 'bowling a googly', 'fielding at silly point' and 'being stumped' are all common cricket terms. It's also perhaps the only sport in the world where the teams stop for a tea break in the afternoon. It's a very gentlemanly game!

We haven't yet mentioned the individual sports that are popular in the UK.

Racquet sports are played a lot. Tennis, badminton, and the exciting, fast-paced indoor game of squash all have competitive leagues.

Water sports are very popular too. Great Britain has some very good conditions for canoeing and kayaking, as well as sailing and rowing. Lots of people swim in the UK so some of the best swimmers in the world compete for Great Britain.

Then there are road sports. Some of the best Formula 1 and rally drivers are British, and cycling is another sport that British people love.

We still haven't talked about athletics! The Great Britain team is always competitive at the Olympics and World athletics championships. Long distance running, like the gruelling marathon event, and the sprinting events are always popular.

The final thing to mention is extreme sports. These are sports that are dangerous, but exciting! Mountain biking, BMX, skateboarding, inline skating and snowboarding are extreme sports. We'll hear some more about these in the chapter on popular children's games.

英国流行的体育运动

郝玉娟 译

  英国的体育运动世界闻名，并孕育了一些世界顶尖的运动员。几乎全世界所有的体育运动在英国都有所开展，所以不管你喜欢何种运动，你都可以在英国找到玩伴。

  世界最古老的足球队（诺茨郡足球俱乐部）和历史最悠久的网球锦标赛（温布尔登）都诞生在英国。

这里还是板球和橄榄球的发源地，也是许多体育运动书面规则的诞生地。

与个人运动相比，团队运动在这里更受欢迎。足球绝对是最流行的团队运动。在很多城镇，在几乎每块空闲的绿地上，你都能发现足球运动员正带球冲过奋力扑救的守门员，力图将球射入球门！

为了说明足球在英国的重要性，20 世纪 60 年代利物浦俱乐部的经理比尔·香克利曾经这样说道："足球不是事关生死，而是高于生死。"对于这句话，很多英国球迷感同身受！

曼联、利物浦、阿森纳和切尔西都是英格兰的顶级球队。想加入这些球队，你必须是世界顶级球员！当然，苏格兰超级联赛中流浪者队和凯尔特人队的一些球员也非常优秀！

像足球一样，橄榄球也是一项风靡英国乃至全世界的团队运动。橄榄球是威尔士的国民运动，他们的球队堪属一流。比赛时，队员投掷并抱着鸡蛋形状的球奔跑，尽力绕开试图追上他们并把他们扑倒在地的对手。橄榄球运动员经常会和其他多名浑身泥泞的球员摔在一起，而橄榄球则被他们压在身下的某个地方。

据说，橄榄球运动诞生在英国的一所学校里：调皮的学生威廉·韦博·埃利斯正在踢足球，但是却并不喜欢；于是他捡起球，撒腿就跑，橄榄球运动由此诞生。

当夏天来临时，橄榄球和足球赛季结束。许多英国人喜欢在这时观看板球比赛。板球比赛有两支队伍参加，属于球类运动。它很受人们欢迎，但若不知道比赛规则，它也会让人感觉混乱不堪。

板球有自己的语言，一些听起来很有趣的词语，如投曲线球、垒外球、持球撞柱等都是常用的板球术语。它可能也是世界上唯一的一项球队会停下比赛喝下午茶的体育运动。这是一种非常绅士的体育运动！

当然，我们也不能漏下英国流行的个人运动。

球拍运动的爱好者众多。网球、羽毛球以及快节奏的室内壁球都有竞争激烈的联赛。

水上运动也很流行。英国具备划独木舟、皮划艇以及开展帆船和划艇运动的优良条件。而大量的游泳爱好者中更是高手辈出，代表英国参加世界大赛。

此外还有公路运动。英国不乏一流的一级方程式和拉力赛车手，当然还有英国人喜爱的自行车运动。

我们还没有谈到田径运动！英国代表队在奥运赛场上和世界田径锦标赛中都具有很强的竞争力。以极为消耗体能的马拉松为代表的长跑以及短跑项目一直很流行。

最后要提到的是极限运动。极限运动危险、刺激，像山地自行车运动、自行车越野赛、滑板运动、滚轴溜冰和单板滑雪都属于这类运动。在本章里，我们还将会更多地了解流行的儿童运动。

Popular sports in the US

Nancy Dickmann

In the United States, for many people sports are a way of life. In the summer, you are sure to see parks full of children and adults playing baseball, soccer (football), or other sports. But all year round, Americans love to play and watch sports.

Baseball

Probably the most popular sport in the US is baseball, which is sometimes called 'the national pastime'. This sport is played by teams of nine players with a bat and a ball. Players take turns trying to hit the ball and run safely around the bases. The rules can be complicated, with unusual terms like 'squeeze play', 'knuckleball', and 'sacrifice fly'.

There are dozens of professional teams, and people turn out by the thousands to watch their local teams play. The most successful team of all time is the New York Yankees. They have won the championship more than 25 times! Softball, a version of baseball played with a slightly bigger ball, is popular with women and children.

American football

If you hear Americans talking about 'football', don't be fooled! They're not talking about soccer—they're talking about American football, a sport that is similar to rugby. Teams try to get the oval ball into the other team's goal by throwing, kicking, or carrying it. Most football players are very tall and strong, but they wear a lot of protective equipment. If you watch a game, you'll understand why! The teams try to stop each other with crunching blocks and tackles.

Professional football teams all want to win one game: the Super Bowl. This game decides the winner of the league, and the nation stops to watch. Most years, the Super Bowl is the most-watched television programme of the year! It is a true spectacle, with famous entertainers performing before the game and during the breaks.

Football played by university students is almost as popular as the professional game. The standard is very high, and many university players go on to play in the professional leagues. At university matches, the crowds are entertained by marching bands and cheerleaders performing energetic routines.

Basketball

Basketball was invented in 1891 as a way to keep fit indoors during the long winters in the northeast United States. Since then, it has become one of the world's most popular sports. Teams of five players try to throw a large round ball through the other team's hoop, or 'basket'. The hoop is 10 feet (3.05 metres) high, so most successful basketball players are very tall!

One of the most famous professional teams is the Chicago Bulls. Michael Jordan played for the Bulls for many years.

Many people enjoy playing basketball. Most parks have at least one basketball court, and you will usually be able to see groups of people 'shooting hoops'.

Ice hockey

One of the fastest-moving team sports in the US is ice hockey. Teams of six players use sticks with flat ends to try to shoot the flat, round puck into the other team's goal. But to make it more difficult, the game is played on ice skates! It is an exciting, fast-paced game, and the puck moves so quickly that it can be difficult to follow! Professional teams from the US and Canada compete to win the Stanley Cup each year.

Soccer

Football (or 'soccer', as Americans call it) is probably the most popular sport around the world, but it has never been one of the top sports in the US. The professional league does not have the same quality players as leagues in other countries, and the matches do not draw huge crowds. However, soccer is very popular among children, and millions of them play on teams. They may be the professional players of the future!

美国的热门体育运动

张华嵩 译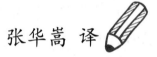

在美国，对于很多人来说，体育运动就是一种生活方式。夏天，你一定会看到公园里挤满了孩子和大人，他们正在打棒球、踢足球或是进行其他体育活动。但是，美国人参与运动和观看体育比赛的热情是不分季节的。

棒球

在美国最受欢迎的运动恐怕要数有"全民娱乐"

之美称的棒球了。两支各九人的球队，一个球棒，一个球，就可以玩儿了。球员依次大力击球，然后奋力跑过四周各垒并安全回到本垒。这一运动的规则有些复杂，涉及"抢分战术""弹指球"和"牺牲腾空球"等不常见的术语。

美国有几十支职业棒球队，成千上万人会赶赴现场观看本地球队的比赛。纽约扬基队是美国有史以来最成功的棒球队，已获得冠军超过 25 次。垒球运动由棒球发展而来，所用球较棒球稍大，是女性和孩子们热衷的运动。

美式足球

如果你听到美国人提起"足球"（football），可不要误解，他们谈的可不是"英式足球"（soccer），而是"美式足球"，一种类似橄榄球的运动。球队通过投球、踢球或带球跑，力争将椭圆形的球送进对方球门。虽然多数美式足球运动员都非常高大健壮，但他们还是会穿戴很多护具。一场比赛看下来，你就会明白个中原因：球员们要以正面阻截和擒抱摔倒阻止对方进攻。

各职业美式足球队都渴望赢得"超级杯"的胜利，这场比赛会最终决定谁是美式足球大联盟的年度赢家。每到这时，人们会停止一切活动来观看比赛。而这场"超级杯"终极决战的电视转播，也几乎成为每年的电视节目收视冠军。"超级杯"决战的现场更是场面壮观，有著名娱乐明星在赛前和赛间休息时进行现场表演。

大学生美式足球比赛的受欢迎程度几乎不亚于职业联赛。大学生球员的水平很高，其中不少球员毕业后会进入职业联盟打球。在大学生足球比赛中，观众还能欣赏到军乐队的演出和啦啦队充满活力的集体舞。

篮球

篮球发明于 1891 年，最初是美国东北部人在漫长冬季里进行室内健身的一种方式。发展到今天，篮球已成为世界范围内最受欢迎的运动之一。五人组成的球队力求把一只大大的圆球投入对方的篮筐。篮筐距离地面 10 英尺（3.05 米），因此出色的球员往往身材非常高大。

最知名的职业篮球队之一是芝加哥公牛队，迈克尔·乔丹就曾为公牛队效力多年。

很多人喜欢打篮球，公园大多设有至少一个篮球场，在那里你总能看到成群的人在投篮。

冰球

在美国，冰球是一项移动速度极快的团体运动。六人的球队使用末梢扁平的球杆力争把扁圆的冰球击入对方球门。冰球的另一大难点在于球员要穿着冰鞋打球。这是一项紧张刺激、快节奏的运动，冰球的快速移动使得跟球跑动异常困难。每年，来自美国和加拿大的职业球队会争夺斯坦利杯。

足球

足球（football，美国人把它称为"soccer"）很可能是全世界最受欢迎的运动，但尚未在美国形成气候。这里的足球职业联赛球员没有其他国家联赛中的球员水平高，比赛也无法吸引大量观众。然而，足球很受孩子们的欢迎，数百万儿童在球队中踢球，而他们可能就是明日的职业球星！

Children's games and sports

James Blanshard

All children love to play, wherever you go in the world. In a school in Britain at playtime, you will see children playing all sorts of games. And after school, if the weather is good and when homework is done, you are sure to find children playing outdoors too.

Everywhere you look in a playground, children are chasing each other! Games of chase are hugely popular in Britain, just like everywhere else in the world. There are lots of types of chase game, and lots of different names for them depending on which part of the UK you visit. 'Tig', 'Tag', or 'Dobby' are all names for the same game. In those games, somebody is 'it' or 'on'. They must chase their friends and try to catch them by slapping or tapping them on the shoulder. When they do they shout "Tig! You're it!"

Do you play a game like tag? There are lots of different types. A very common tag game is 'dobby scarecrow'. When a player is tagged they must stand with their legs apart in a star shape, like a scarecrow.

If a free player crawls between their legs they are released to keep playing, but if the player or players that are 'it' turn everybody into scarecrows, then they win!

There is one game of tag that can be played by the whole school! British bulldog is a tag game that often involves lots of players. In British bulldog, a group of players line up on one side of a playing field or playground and they have to run to the other side. But it isn't that simple... in the middle of the field stand the bulldogs. Their task is to catch the runners and tag them, turning them into bulldogs too. The game is over either when the bulldogs have caught everybody, or there is one person left, who is declared the winner! British bulldog can be quite a physical game, and because it is played over a big area, it can take up a lot of space. For these reasons, some schools don't allow it.

One of the best things about tag games is you don't need any extra equipment, like a bat or ball to play. Some games though do need equipment. Ball games are always popular, and wherever you look in the UK you will find children playing football. Often, if there are no goalposts to use, children will use their jumpers or coats as goalposts instead. This often means they get muddy, which is sure to upset whoever does the laundry at home!

Another popular piece of kit that is found in many playgrounds is a skipping rope. Children take it in turns skipping into the swinging rope and jumping, while a rhyme is chanted. One common rhyme goes like this:

Apples, peaches, pears and plums
Tell me when your birthday comes.

The people turning the rope then swing it really fast while chanting the months of the year—January, February, March, April...—and the skippers must jump out when their birthday month is called. If you are born in December that means you might get very tired!

At the weekends, when there is lots of time to play, many boys and girls enjoy skating and skateboarding. Most towns have skate parks, which are places where there are ramps and rails for doing tricks. Riding bikes is fun too. BMX bikes are great for doing tricks and jumps, and some towns have special tracks for people to race or practise tricks at.

Whatever types of game you like to play, there are lots to choose from. If you don't feel like playing one of these games we've mentioned, why not try to think of your own tag game, or invent a new ball game?

儿童游戏和运动

张华嵩 译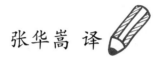

世界上任何地方的孩子们都喜欢玩儿。在任何一所英国学校，你都可以看到孩子们在游戏时间玩各种各样的游戏。放学之后，只要天气不错，功课已完成，你肯定能看到孩子们在室外玩耍。

环顾一下操场，你会看到到处都是追逐嬉戏的孩子！与世界其他地方一样，捉人游戏在英国也非常受欢迎。英国流行的捉人游戏有很多种，而且在英国不同的地方，捉人游戏的名字会有所不同，比如"滴答"（Tig 或 Tag）或"杜比"（Dobby）其实都是指捉人游戏。在这些游戏中，有个孩子是追人者，他要尽力追赶其他小伙伴，一旦追上，拍下他们的肩膀就算追赶成功，此时，追人者要喊"捉到你啦！"

你玩过类似"滴答"的捉人游戏吗？这种游戏还包括很多类型。有一种常见的捉人游戏叫做"杜比稻草人"。玩游戏的人一旦被抓到就必须双腿分开呈星形站立，姿势就如同一个站立的稻草人。如果有行动自由的游戏者从"稻草人"两腿间爬过，这个"稻草人"

就可以恢复自由、继续玩游戏。但是，当一个或多个追人者把其他人都变成"稻草人"之后，追人者就成为胜利的一方！

有一种捉人的游戏可以使整个学校的学生参与其中！"英国喇叭狗"是一种参加人数众多的捉人游戏。在这种游戏中，一队参与者在操场的一端站成一排，他们需要跑到操场的另一端。但这个游戏并非如此简单。追人者会站在操场中间，他们的任务就是捉到被追者之后将其变成追人者。当追人者追到所有的被追者，游戏就结束了。或者仅剩一个人没有被追到时，此人就是游戏的胜利者！"英国喇叭狗"是个耗费体力的游戏，而且这种游戏所需的场地也很大。正是由于这些原因，有些学校不允许开展这项游戏。

玩捉人游戏的好处之一是不需要特别准备器械，比如球拍或球。然而有些游戏却需要器械。球类运动在英国一直很受欢迎，无论走到哪里，你都可以看到孩子们在踢足球。如果没有门柱，孩子们通常情况下会用毛衣或外套来充当门柱。这就意味着衣服会变得很脏，这恐怕会使家里洗衣服的人十分郁闷！

操场上常见的另一种受欢迎的体育用品是跳绳。孩子们反复吟唱着儿歌，轮流跳进正在摆动的绳子并不断跳跃。一首常见的儿歌是这样唱的：

苹果、桃子、梨子和李子，请告诉我你生日的日子。

吟唱月份的时候，负责摇绳子的人会把绳子摇得很快，如1月、2月、3月、4月……喊到谁的生日月份，谁就必须立即跳出来。如此一来，要是你出生在12月，可就要累坏啦！

周末玩的时间比较充裕，很多男孩子和女孩子喜欢玩滑冰和滑板。大多数的城镇都有滑冰场，在这些场地里有练习技巧用的坡道和轨道。骑自行车也同样有趣。自行车越野赛使用的自行车可以做出很炫的技巧和跳跃动作。有些城镇有比赛专用车道和练习技巧所需的车道。

不论你喜欢玩哪种游戏，总有很多游戏供你选择。如果你不喜欢玩我们提到的游戏，为什么不自己试着发明一种捉人游戏，或是一种新的球类游戏呢？

Fun indoors

James Blanshard

If it's a rainy day and you're stuck at home, what can you do? Fortunately, rainy days happen so often in the UK that British people have become experts at keeping busy indoors!

Video games are very popular in the UK. Many children own a game console or play games on their home computer. However, not all parents like their children to play video games, so this is often only done as a treat. The same applies to watching TV.

Indoors isn't a great place to run around, so board games are very handy to have around for rainy days. You can find all sorts of these in toy shops. Have you ever played the trading game Monopoly, the murder mystery game Cluedo, or Snakes and Ladders? In these games you have to roll the dice and move your playing pieces around a board.

Some of the most popular board games are very old. The game of English draughts (also called American checkers) is very popular in the UK and America. In draughts, two players take turns to try to move their playing pieces diagonally to the opposite side of the board. They must try to jump their pieces over their opponent's pieces to capture them.

The same checked board is used to play chess. Chess dates back hundreds of years. It is a complicated two-player game in which the players have to try to capture the opponent's pieces. Chess games can take many hours to play, but they are very popular. There are even international chess tournaments!

Scrabble is a different type of board game that is played all over the world. It is a game of luck and skill, and it's also a good game for learning to spell! Each player picks seven tiles out of a bag. The tiles have letters of the English alphabet on them. The players must take it in turns to try to make words from their tiles and build a crossword puzzle on the board. Long and difficult words lead to higher scores!

Other games that are very popular in the UK and US are Jenga, where you have to build a tower using building blocks, and dominos, which is a game played with numbered tiles. Have you ever played those games?

But if you don't have a board game handy, there are still games you can play.

A popular word game that you can play anywhere with a pencil and paper is Hangman. This is a game for two players in which one thinks of a word and the other has to guess what it is by choosing letters. If the guessing player chooses a letter that is not in the word, the first player draws part of a picture of a hanging man! When the picture is complete, the drawing player wins, so the guessing player must do their best to guess the word as quickly as they can.

When board and card games just aren't energetic enough, hide and seek is always a fun option. You need at least two players to play hide and seek. The seeker closes their eyes while the hider tries to find somewhere to hide. The seeker counts up to 20 or another agreed number, shouting as they count so that the hider knows how much longer they have to find a good hiding place.

When the seeker has finished counting they shout, "Here I come, ready or not!" then sets off to find the hiding player. Sometimes there's a time limit, so that the hiding player wins if the seeker doesn't find them in time.

What sorts of games do you like playing at home? Do you like board games like chess, word games like scrabble, or more active games like hide and seek? There's always something fun to do.

有趣的室内活动

韩淑俊 译

　　如果外面下雨，你只能呆在家里，那么能做些什么呢？所幸的是，虽然英国经常下雨，但是英国人在开展室内活动方面已经变得极为在行。

　　电子游戏在英国非常流行。许多儿童都有自己的游戏机或是电脑来玩游戏，但并非所有的家长都赞同自己的孩子打电子游戏。和允许看电视一样，通常情况下玩电子游戏只是一种奖励。

　　室内并不适合奔跑，因此在雨天玩棋类游戏倒是不错。你可以在玩具店买到你所喜欢的各种棋类。你有没有玩过"大富翁""妙探寻凶"或"蛇梯棋"？这些游戏需要你掷骰子并在棋盘上移动标记位置的棋子。

　　有些最流行的棋类游戏可是有不少年头了。跳棋游戏在英国和美国都很流行。玩跳棋的时候，玩家轮番沿对角方向移动棋子到棋盘的另一端。玩家必须跳过对方的棋子才能吃掉它们。

　　同样的棋盘可以用来下象棋。象棋的历史可以追溯到数百年前。玩这种复杂的双人游戏时，玩家必须设法吃掉对方的棋子。一盘棋可能要下很长时间，却非常受欢迎。甚至还有很多国际象棋锦标赛！

拼字游戏是另一种风靡全世界的棋盘类游戏。这种游戏需要运气和技巧，同时也是一个学习拼写的不错的游戏。每个玩家从一个袋子里取出七张英文字母牌，依次尝试着用它们拼出单词并在棋盘上建造一个纵横字谜。长而难的单词可以获取高分。

在英美国家深受喜爱的游戏还包括积木游戏层层叠（Jenga）和多米诺骨牌（dominos）。玩层层叠时，你要用积木建一座塔；而多米诺骨牌则是一种用编了号的牌玩的游戏。你玩过这些游戏吗？

但如果你手头没有这样的棋类游戏，你还可以尝试一下其他的游戏。

吊死鬼游戏是一种只需要纸和笔随时随地都可以玩的猜字游戏。这种游戏需要两个玩家，一个玩家想出一个单词，另一个玩家则需要通过选择字母猜出这个单词。如果猜词者给出错误的字母，对方就会画出一个被吊着的小人儿的一部分。当"被吊的小人儿"所有笔画完成，给词的一方就赢了。因此，猜词的一方必须尽快猜出这个单词。

如果你觉得棋类和纸牌类游戏不带劲儿的话，捉迷藏总是一个不错的选择。捉迷藏至少需要两个参与者。在追捕者闭上眼睛后，藏的人要找地方躲起来。追捕者数到20或一个双方商定好的数字，并且数数时声音要洪亮，以便让藏的人知道他还剩多少时间来寻找合适的藏身地。

追捕者数完数后会喊："我要来找你了！准备好了吗？"他就开始行动了。有时还有时间上的限制。如果追捕者在限定的时间内没能找到藏的人，那么藏的人就胜利了。

你喜欢在家里玩什么样的游戏呢？是喜欢象棋之类的棋类游戏，拼字游戏这样的文字游戏，还是捉迷藏一类更活跃点儿的游戏呢？当然，总有一些好玩儿的游戏可以做。